DAN ISSEL

Praise for *Dan Issel: From Kentucky Wildcat to NBA Legend*

"As a young basketball fan, I distinctly remember Dan Issel dominating NBA scoring wearing that iconic rainbow Nuggets jersey. When I became a player for the University of Kentucky, I grew to understand and admire how beloved he truly is by Big Blue Nation. And now as head coach I can proudly say he and his beautiful wife, Cheri, have become friends. 'The Horse' had an unmatched hall of fame career for both the Wildcats and in the NBA, and I know fans will appreciate discovering and reliving his incredible journey to become one of the best to ever play the game."—Mark Pope, head coach, University of Kentucky men's basketball

"Dan Issel was always ready to play up to the hype. He could score, rebound, and lead with a fundamental game that made teammates better and secured his place in the Naismith Memorial Basketball Hall of Fame. It is my honor to salute him and share in his glory. His combined ABA/NBA numbers warrant inspection and acceptance, making him one of the greatest to ever play pro basketball. Thank you, Dan, and job well done."—Julius "Dr. J." Erving, ABA and NBA legend and Naismith Memorial Basketball Hall of Fame inductee

"I first met Dan Issel as he was just beginning his UK basketball career, as a 'kitten,' a wide-eyed freshman. Little could either of us realize that this late blooming player was taking the first steps of a hall of fame career. Dan would become not only UK's all-time leading men's scorer but also one of the most prolific point getters in the history of professional basketball. Often matched against taller rivals, Dan succeeded with hustle, shooting ability, and durability. Following his playing days, Dan would have notable careers as an NBA coach, Thoroughbred owner and breeder, television commentor, and businessman. With so many accomplishments, though, there were rough times too. Now, in *Dan Issel: From Kentucky Wildcat to NBA Legend,* all the details of the highs and lows are revealed. What ultimately emerges is Dan's faith and his innate goodness. This book is a must-read for Big Blue Nation and basketball fans everywhere."—Tom Hammond, author of *Races, Games, and Olympic Dreams: A Sportscaster's Life*

"I've always admired Dan's achievements in the basketball world, but what stands out even more is his deep faith and unwavering commitment to family and friends—qualities that shine throughout this book."—Louie Dampier, former Kentucky Wildcats point guard, former assistant coach of the Denver Nuggets, and Naismith Memorial Basketball Hall of Famer

"Dan Issel's basketball life spans several of the most significant topics in the sport's history—Coach Rupp, the legendary ABA, and the NBA's evolution from perhaps a distant third of the major leagues into a worldwide athletic powerhouse. He is sometimes overlooked in favor of flashier players or personalities, but this new release gives Issel an excellent chance to tell the inside story."—Joe Cox, coauthor of *Voice of the Wildcats: Claude Sullivan and the Rise of Modern Sportscasting*

"When I think of the best player ever to wear the blue and white, I immediately think of Dan Issel! He muscled and hustled his way into college basketball lore at the University of Kentucky, becoming the school's all-time leading scorer for men's basketball. After our basketball days ended, I got to know Dan off the court—and I was pleasantly surprised to learn that he's an even better person than he was a player. . . . I'm thankful for all that Dan did to help build UK basketball into the premier college basketball program in the country. Dan, Kenny 'Sky' Walker, and I share the distinct honor of being the only three players in UK basketball history to have scored two thousand points in our careers. . . . Dan accomplished this in just three seasons, while it took Kenny and me four. That's why he's the best!"—Jack "Goose" Givens, former UK basketball star, 1978 Final Four Most Outstanding Player, author of *They Call Me Goose: My Life in Kentucky Basketball and Beyond*, and radio color analyst for the UK Sports Network

"Author Doug Brunk has done it again, this time teaming up with my Big Blue brother, Dan Issel, to create this beautifully written memoir. Dan may be a basketball champion, but I have always known him as a wonderful person. We share a unique relationship as a trivia question: 'Who is the University of Kentucky's all-time leading scorer?' *Dan Issel: From Kentucky Wildcat to NBA Legend* sheds light on Dan's unique position in the development of basketball, from UK to the ABA to the NBA. It's a must-read for anyone who loves history and basketball."—Valerie Still, UK's all-time leading scorer in basketball, former WNBA standout, and author of the forthcoming *Still Family: William Still and the Legacy of the Underground Railroad*

DAN ISSEL

FROM **KENTUCKY WILDCAT** TO **NBA LEGEND**

DAN ISSEL

with Doug Brunk

Foreword by Hannah Storm

UNIVERSITY PRESS OF KENTUCKY

Scholarly publisher for the Commonwealth, serving Bellarmine University, Berea College, Centre College of Kentucky, Eastern Kentucky University, The Filson Historical Society, Georgetown College, Kentucky Historical Society, Kentucky State University, Morehead State University, Murray State University, Northern Kentucky University, Simmons College, Spalding University, Transylvania University, University of Kentucky, University of Louisville, University of Pikeville, and Western Kentucky University.

Editorial and Sales Offices: The University Press of Kentucky
663 South Limestone, Lexington, Kentucky 40508-4008
www.kentuckypress.com

Unless otherwise noted, photographs are from the author's collection.

Cataloging-in-Publication data available from the Library of Congress

ISBN 978-1-9859-0520-7 (hardcover)
ISBN 978-1-9859-0521-4 (paperback)
ISBN 978-1-9859-0522-1 (pdf)
ISBN 978-1-9859-0523-8 (epub)

ASSOCIATION of UNIVERSITY PRESSES
Member of the Association of University Presses

To my wife, Cheri—my partner through all these years,
and still the prettiest cheerleader in Kentucky.

Do not be anxious about anything, but in everything, by prayer and petition, with thanksgiving, present your requests to God. And the peace of God, which transcends all understanding, will guard your hearts and minds in Christ Jesus.

PHILIPPIANS 4:6–7, NEW INTERNATIONAL VERSION

NEW BRUNSWICK, N.J.: INTERNATIONAL BIBLE SOCIETY, 1978

Contents

Foreword

I have known Dan Issel just about my whole life—from my journey with my dad, Mike Storen, through the ABA and then my own through the NBA. Both of those leagues were super important to Dan, and he was equally important to them.

My dad was the president and general manager of the Kentucky Colonels, and I first remember Dan as a larger-than-life presence in our home. Sometimes the players would come over for an event like a Christmas party. I remember my mom making homemade ornaments with the Colonels logo for them to take home. At the time I was just a grade school kid, pretty oblivious to who these very tall people were, except that they worked with my dad!

Having played at the University of Kentucky and for the Kentucky Colonels, Dan was a local hero. It was my dad's idea to change the team's colors from green and black to blue and white, in honor of Dan and his Kentucky stardom, along with former UK players Louie Dampier and Mike Pratt.

Dad was a big promoter, inviting players from local men's leagues to play preliminary games to help build the Colonels' crowds at Freedom Hall. He would give tickets to cab drivers and barbers in the hope that they would help get the word out about the team, and he loved sitting in the locker room and talking to the players. It was a *huge* deal that Dan signed with the Colonels and not the NBA.

Dan was physical and gritty to be sure, but above all he was an offensive force—a scoring machine! The all-time leading scorer at Kentucky, he went on to become the ABA's second all-time leading scorer and, as of this writing, ranks third on the Denver Nuggets' all-time scoring list. He was one of the most durable players in basketball, hence his nickname "The Horse." Dan helped the Colonels to a championship in the 1974–75 season alongside Artis Gilmore and Louie Dampier, which was just about the most exciting thing that had ever happened to our family!

I would follow in my dad's footsteps and pursue the world of basketball as my profession. Growing up around the game made me comfortable in that space—one in which there were no women when I started out.

One of the coolest things that happened early in my broadcasting career was reuniting with Dan Issel when he was coach of the Nuggets, leading them to their first winning record and the playoffs for the first time in four years. I was the courtside reporter for NBC when the Nuggets became the first ever eighth seed to knock off a number one seed in the first round, and they did it after getting into an 0–2 hole! I remember having to step back out of the famous shot when Dikembe Mutombo was on the floor cradling the basketball before interviewing him. It was so cool to go through that experience with Dan as the coach. It made me so comfortable, and I really felt like my life had come full circle.

I'm so honored that Dan asked me to write the foreword for this memoir. He's such an important figure in the world of basketball, and in my world as well! Enjoy!

Hannah Storm
ESPN anchor and award-winning journalist

Preface

I first met my coauthor, Doug Brunk, when he drove from San Diego to my office at Bel Air Presbyterian Church in Los Angeles in 2012 to interview me for his first book, *Wildcat Memories.* Since then, I've read two more of his works—*Forty Minutes to Glory* and *They Call Me Goose*—so I knew going into this project that anything Doug worked on would be a high-quality product.

Still, I had some hesitation. I didn't want this to turn into a feel-good Facebook post where everything is just "wonderful." I knew that if I wanted to be authentic, I'd have to revisit some darker times in my life. I wasn't sure I was ready to go there. But in the end, I agreed to take this journey with Doug for two reasons. First, I wanted to leave something for my grandkids and great-grandkids, a way for them to truly understand what kind of person I was. And second, I wanted to show others that when life knocks you down, it's always better to get back up than to wallow in self-pity or feel like a victim. I was fortunate to grow up in a religious, loving family that instilled blue-collar values and a blue-collar work ethic.

My favorite statistic isn't about the number of points I scored or rebounds I grabbed. It's the fact that I never missed a single basketball game in junior high, high school, or college. And in fifteen years of professional basketball, I only missed twenty-four games. I wasn't always great, wasn't even always good, but I showed up and gave it everything I had.

As you'll read in the following pages, I was fortunate to play for some legendary coaches—Hall of Famers like Don Vandersnick, Adolph Rupp, Larry Brown, Frank Ramsey, Hubie Brown, and Doug Moe. Choosing to attend the University of Kentucky (UK) was the best decision I ever made. Not only did I get to play for the iconic Coach Rupp, who pushed and inspired me, but I also met the prettiest cheerleader in the state—Cheri Hughes—who has been my wife since 1969.

Staying in Kentucky to play for the Colonels of the American Basketball Association (ABA) felt like an extension of my college career. The highlight of my basketball life came more than fifty years ago, on May 22, 1975, when the Colonels won the ABA championship in Freedom Hall. Not long after, I was sold—not traded—to the Denver Nuggets via the Baltimore Claws. At the time, it felt like the worst thing that could happen. But God had a plan. A year later, the ABA folded, the Colonels were gone, and the Nuggets were one of only four ABA teams that merged into the NBA.

After playing my final professional game in 1985, my dream of retiring to Courtland Farm in Versailles, Kentucky, only lasted three years. As you'll see, there were reasons for that. I later became an NBA coach with zero coaching experience. One of the proudest moments of my career was leading the 1993–94 Nuggets to the playoffs and upsetting the Seattle SuperSonics in the first round.

But not everything was a success story.

On December 11, 2001, I made a terrible remark in the heat of the moment, something I deeply regret to this day. That moment brought shame on me, my family, and my fans. We'll talk about that in this book, and about the grace, forgiveness, and resilience that followed.

Then came June 30, 2009, the darkest day of my life. I declared bankruptcy at sixty-one after becoming overextended and lost everything. That experience taught me a lesson I'll never forget: don't borrow money you can't pay back, and don't invest in what you don't control. Since that day, I haven't borrowed a dime. And I sleep better at night.

Today, in the twilight of our lives, Cheri and I are happier and more content than we've ever been. We were blessed to recover and rebuild.

In 1993, I was inducted into the Naismith Memorial Basketball Hall of Fame, an incredible honor and the ultimate individual recognition for anyone who plays, coaches, or officiates the game. I was part of one of the greatest Hall of Fame classes ever, and that meant the world to me. But honestly, the decision to attend UK changed my life even more. Decades later, I can still walk the streets of Lexington and be greeted like I just played last night. The love and passion of Kentucky basketball fans are unlike anything else in the world. I believe I played for the greatest college basketball program—and in front of the greatest fans—in the country.

To the young reader who might be sitting on the bench right now, or wondering if you'll ever get your shot: don't give up. I was a late bloomer myself. But I had people—like my high school coach, Don Vandersnick—who believed in me. If you're passionate about something, chase it with everything you've got. You may not be the starter or the star right away, or even ever, but if you work hard and stay the course, anything is possible.

Dan Issel
Highlands Ranch, Colorado

1

The Fields I Knew

Growing up, farming was all I knew. Until I was four, I lived on a 160-acre dairy farm in Batavia, Illinois, owned by my maternal grandparents, Ida and Henry Meyer. A long driveway led from the main road to a big, two-story farmhouse my grandparents lived in. There were three other homes within a stone's throw of theirs: two that housed two sets of aunts and uncles, and a third that was home to my parents, Robert and Eleanor Issel, when they welcomed me into the world on October 25, 1948, about eleven months after they married. I was their first child, and my birth weight was more like that of a bowling ball, tipping the scales at twelve pounds, eleven ounces. This caused some hospital staff to joke that I would be walking home from the hospital. When they cleared me and Mom to go home, my parents named me Daniel Paul Issel, after the main character in the Book of Daniel and Paul the Apostle, which I thought was cool.

I don't remember much about those first four years in Batavia, but our small, three-bedroom house started to feel cramped after my siblings were born—Kathi the following year and Greg two years after me.

My parents got married right out of high school. Neither attended college, but they provided a great atmosphere for us. My grandparents did, too. They and my parents raised us in a traditional Lutheran Church, which taught us that people are saved by God's grace through faith alone, and that God's love is unconditional. We attended services together every Sunday and said a prayer before each meal: "Come, Lord Jesus, be our

Mom and Dad holding me in front of our house at 711 College Street in Batavia, Illinois—a number often seen as a sign of divine support.

guest. Let these gifts to us be blessed. Amen." My family and I continue to recite that prayer to this day.

I was blessed to grow up in a close-knit family filled with love. We were considered lower middle class. Although we didn't have much, everyone worked hard, especially my dad. He was a house painter by trade, just a good, solid, blue-collar type. He fit the Midwestern stereotype of being reserved and had an easygoing temperament, but when you did something wrong, he wasn't opposed to disciplining you. I didn't get a lot of whippings as a kid, but one time there was a hog in grandma and grandpa's barn that was getting ready to have a litter. When I was just three or four years old, I walked to the barn by myself, grabbed a bushel of corn, and fed that mother hog. When Dad found out, I got a pretty good whipping, because you never give a hog a whole bushel of corn at once.

Though Dad was a loving and hardworking father, his own childhood was far from easy, and that experience shaped how he raised us. I never learned the full story, but Dad's mother passed away either during his birth or shortly afterward. Soon after that, Dad moved in with an aunt and uncle. Then his dad remarried and had two daughters with his new wife. I wouldn't describe my dad as a cast out, but I don't think he had a great childhood in terms of his relationship with his father and stepmom. As a result, he was determined to ensure that his kids had a much better childhood than he did.

Mom was a traditional Lutheran, a devoted Christian, and a strong German mother who made sure we behaved, but always in a loving and caring way. She wasn't mean; she just ensured we did the right thing. I always admired her for that. For example, she never missed a Parent Teacher Association meeting or a teacher's conference. She also seemed to know what her kids were up to in and out of the classroom. If she liked you, there was nothing she wouldn't do for you. But if you got on her bad side, it was best to stay out of her way.

Like Mom, Grandma and Grandpa Meyer also had a strong sense of duty and faith, and their influence really shaped my understanding of family and responsibility. They were a hardworking, responsible German couple who never slacked off. They also took their Christian faith seriously. If you weren't in church, Grandma would knock on the door by noon wanting to know who was sick.

While my parents and grandparents worked on their farm, two of my uncles, who owned farms in Central Missouri, were reaping a plentiful

My maternal grandparents, Ida and Henry Meyer, who were the spiritual heart of our family.

harvest in the "Show-Me" state. It was like the story in the Bible, where Pharaoh dreamed that seven skinny cows emerged from the river and feasted on seven fat cows. Their farms were doing very well. Envious of their success, my parents and grandparents chose to leave Batavia behind for a farming life in Missouri, hoping to achieve the same prosperity. So did my aunts and uncles. This time, each family would have its own farm and no longer share the same property, yet we ended up living within about five miles of each other. That shows just how close our family was.

Since my siblings and I were so young, none of us felt a strong emotional attachment to Batavia, so the move to Missouri wasn't a big deal. We settled on a dairy farm in rural Green Ridge, which is in Pettis County. The existing house had no electricity or running water, so adjusting to that—and to using an outhouse—took some getting used to. The first place on the farm to have electricity and running water was the dairy barn my dad built, which included a large, metal barrel. My siblings and I took many baths in that barrel! I was too little to do any of the milking; my job was to take care of the calves. One I bonded to was named Sally. Kathi, Greg, and I often took turns riding her around like a pony.

Living on a farm, we didn't have the option of walking down the block to play with other kids, so my siblings and I became each other's best friends and playmates. Kathi was more introverted, and it took her much longer than usual to start talking. My parents were concerned and even had her hearing tested. Eventually, her doctor concluded that she wasn't talking because I was speaking for her! Greg was the more outgoing one. As the older brother, I was always incredibly protective of both Kathi and Greg. Greg and I shared a lot in common, which made our bond even stronger.

Since Green Ridge had no kindergarten, I started first grade when I was just five years old. Classes were held in a one-building schoolhouse: the elementary grades were on the first floor, sixth through eighth were upstairs, and the high school was on the top floor.

The school bus didn't come directly to our farm. It stopped about a mile away, at the intersection of two gravel roads. On the first day of school, Mom wanted me to ride the bus so I could learn how it all worked. She planned to follow the bus in the car and be there when I got off, since I had no idea where I was going or what to expect. We drove up to the crossroads to wait for the bus, but then Mom realized she had to use the

At Green Ridge with our calf, Sally, a moment captured from those early days.

bathroom. She left me standing by the side of the road while she drove back to the house. While she was gone, the bus arrived.

The driver opened the door, and I got on, completely clueless. Thankfully, Mom caught up with the bus by the time it reached the school. She helped me exit the bus and find my way to first grade. I used to have a photograph from that day. I was wearing a full denim outfit: blue jean jacket, matching pants, and a cowboy hat!

Just to show how deeply rooted Mom's religious faith was, she led devotions every morning at breakfast with me, Kathi, and Greg. She believed it was the best way to start the day. These devotions consisted of reading from Lutheran guideposts and reciting The Lord's Prayer before we headed off to school.

From left: Greg, Kathi, and me. I was about eight years old in this photograph.

The Lutheran church we attended served communion every Sunday. If Mom went to a service where communion wasn't offered, she didn't feel like she had truly been to church. She loved the sound of the organ and the old hymns and didn't care much for guitars and drums in a worship service. That traditional view of faith and worship influenced our whole family.

Every year at Christmas, we'd attend the Christmas Eve service. After church, we'd head home, but Mom and Dad would have us kids wait in the car for about twenty minutes while they went inside to arrange all the gifts under the tree. They told us that Santa had a lot of houses to visit, but he always came to ours first. We believed that story for a long, long time. Once everything was set up, they'd come back out to the car, bring us inside, and we'd open our gifts.

While taking square dancing lessons, my parents became close friends with three other couples from Green Ridge and nearby Sedalia: John and Bev Harvey, George and Betty Whitman, and Jay and June Rissler. Together with their children, these couples became our family's core social circle, and we spent a lot of time together.

Back then, you could buy fireworks in Missouri, so every Fourth of July all four families would gather at someone's farm for a big picnic. We'd grill hamburgers and hot dogs and serve all the classic sides: potato salad, baked beans, and coleslaw. Between the four families, there were ten of us kids running around, having a blast. After dinner, the dads would put on our own fireworks show. I remember those celebrations so clearly. They were a real highlight of my early childhood.

Green Ridge was a tiny community, the kind of place where every able-bodied boy was expected to try out for the Little League team, so that's what I did. I don't recall having ever seen a baseball game before, so I had no expectations. I didn't make the team, but the coaches said I could still be part of it, though I wouldn't receive a uniform. There I was, sitting on the bench in my blue jeans and white T-shirt. I felt discouraged, but I chose to focus on my responsibilities on the farm. In fact, if you look at pictures of me from that time, you'll notice I always had iron-on patches on my pants from spending so much time on my knees playing farm. My earliest aspiration was to become a farmer.

Our family's first few years on the farm were rough. It hardly rained, so the crops were weak. Dad had to join a local house painting company to help make ends meet. We never went hungry, though. We raised pigs and cows, and every spring we'd go to the feed store to buy a box of one hundred baby chicks, which we raised through the summer. I still remember when my Uncle Marvin, a butcher by trade, would come down to help us process them. In just one day, we'd butcher all one hundred chickens.

It might sound a little gruesome, but we had a big log out back, and we'd use a hatchet to decapitate the chickens right there. I can still picture my mom, her apron speckled with blood, working tirelessly alongside us. Those one hundred chickens were a big part of getting us through the winter.

Every summer, Mom planted a huge garden and spent countless hours canning. Raising a growing family on the farm, both she and Dad worked incredibly hard, and nearly everything we ate was something we had raised or grown ourselves.

Since I didn't compete in sports, I decided to enter some of our heifers in local 4-H livestock competitions. I didn't win any blue or red ribbons, but I did receive a ribbon of some color, which was still important to me. Another contest I participated in had nothing to do with cows. One year, Mom drove me, Kathi, Greg, and my cousins to the Missouri State

Sharing a funny moment with Mom by the outhouse at Green Ridge.

Fair in Sedalia. As we walked around, she spotted a sign that advertised a competition in four categories: Best Baby Girl, Best Baby Boy, Best Girl, and Best Boy, with winners chosen at the end of the fair. For some reason, mom signed me up for the event. Judges performed a brief physical exam on the contestants, checking our heart rate, teeth, and body weight. A few weeks later, I received a medal in the mail: my prize for winning the Best Boy contest! Evidently, I was in pretty good health from the very beginning.

When I was six or seven years old, Dad built a new house on the farm, one with electricity and running water. When he put the subflooring down, he drew a chalk line where the studs were, and I hammered nails into the subflooring along that chalk line. I developed a strong work ethic on the farm by performing tasks like these. Other times I'd help on my grandparents' farm, which had a large hayfield. One day, Grandpa and my uncles were loading hay bales onto a flatbed truck. Once they had a full load, they drove the truck to the barn to store the bales. Grandpa placed me behind the steering wheel, pulled out the choke, and I steered the truck between the bales of hay on the way to the barn. I couldn't have been more than ten years old. I don't think my parents ever found out about that! Meanwhile, Grandma Ida and I bonded over watching horse races on the television. Grandma would place a bet or two with a bookmaker she knew in Chicago. I remember watching the 1958 Kentucky Derby with her on a small television set in their farmhouse. Tim Tam, a three-year-old colt from Calumet Farm in Lexington, Kentucky, won that race.

Farming life generally felt like a good fit for me, but I became aware of its possible risks. On Saturday mornings, Mom would pack us into the car and drive us to the grocery store in Sedalia, about nine miles away from our farm. I disliked going on those Saturday morning trips, so I usually managed to talk my way out of them by offering to stay behind and help Dad with his farm work. On one of those Saturdays, Dad was breaking up the soil with a disc harrow and he let me ride on the back of the tractor while he steered it down the field. I was probably six years old. While we were rumbling along, I fell off the back of the tractor, and one of the harrow's metal discs ran over my head. Dad didn't realize what had happened until he reached the end of the field, turned around, and saw me on the ground with a bloody head. He scooped me up and ran about half a mile to the farm of our neighbors, the Hoards, and they drove me to the hospital in Sedalia. I didn't pass out, but I remember there being a lot of blood on my jacket. I needed sixty-four stitches on the top of my

With my siblings on the cistern by our Green Ridge farmhouse. I'm the tall one in the group.

head and was hospitalized for several days. The cut started at the top of my forehead and went back across the crown of my head. As soon as they took the stitches out, I was fine.

The ongoing drought conditions in Central Missouri meant there wasn't enough grass for our cattle to graze on, and our crops didn't do well. My parents grew tired of the farm's slim profit margins, so at the end of my fifth-grade school year our family moved back to Batavia, which had a population of about seventy-five hundred. We rented a house on the east side of the city. That summer I fell in love with the Chicago Cubs and their shortstop Ernie Banks, my first childhood sports hero. Before Wrigley Field had lights, WGN-TV in Chicago televised home daytime games, so I became hooked. Ernie was the home run hitter, the undisputed star of the team. Known for his saying, "Let's play two," Ernie often wore a smile on his face; he seemed to enjoy what he was doing. That made an impression on me. He was Major League Baseball's Most Valuable Player two years in a row (1958 and 1959), a testament to his domination in the sport. My first athletic dream was to play shortstop for the Cubs.

The following summer, my parents bought a house on the west side, where I began seventh grade with new classmates at Grace McWayne Elementary School. On the first day, an announcement came across the school PA system inviting anyone who wanted to try out for the football team to meet in the gym locker room after classes ended. I figured this would be a good way to make friends, though I knew nothing about the sport. When I arrived, they were handing out shoulder pads, football pants, and other gear. I had no idea how to put this stuff on, so I got dressed by mimicking what other guys did. We gathered on the football field, and the coach, Ken Swanson, said, "Now men, we're going to start with the basics. Is there anybody here who doesn't know how many men are on a football team?" The guys around me started to laugh, thinking it was a good joke, but I had no clue. I went home and looked it up in our encyclopedia and discovered that a football team can only field eleven players at any given time.

I earned a spot on the football team and played tight end—poorly. I had a uniform this time, but I didn't play much. Because Batavia was so small, almost all able-bodied boys and girls had to participate in all sports to field a team. I played football, basketball, baseball, and a little bit of track (high hurdles), but I wasn't good at any of them early on.

After football season, I tried out for the seventh-grade basketball team and somehow made the roster. I was five feet, four inches tall, but like with football, I didn't play much. Our games started at four o'clock, right after school. On game days, Dad would arrive at work an hour early so he could leave an hour early to watch our team, even though I rarely got off the bench. One thing I'll always remember is the unwavering support I received from my family. Around that time, Dad put up a basketball hoop above our garage so I could practice at home. Greg and I played hours of one-on-one games there in all kinds of weather.

One of my best friends in seventh grade was Teddy Bachand. His mom was a huge Cubs fan, and starting the summer after seventh grade she'd pile a bunch of us into the car four or five times each summer and take us to Wrigley Field.

My dad would hand me a $5 bill. Bleacher seats were $1.50, and with the rest I could get a Coke and a hot dog. So, not only did I watch almost every game that summer on WGN, I also got to go to four or five of them in person. And it was perfect.

While sports were a big part of my life during that time, Mom also encouraged me and my siblings to explore other interests, so she hired Evelyn Panky, the organist at our church, to give us piano lessons. We had an upright piano, and Miss Panky came to our house for individual lessons with me, Kathi, and Greg. If you hit the wrong notes, she would smack your knuckles with her pencil! After about two years of knuckle raps and little progress on the piano, Mom and Dad realized that I wasn't cut out for it, so they let me quit my lessons.

Although my attempts at musical talent had ended, my next experience with physical activity would prove to be just as painful, though more dramatic. On the first day of eighth grade, I showed up for gym class and the teacher had us run laps around the basketball court, which had just been waxed. As I turned a corner, my feet slipped out from under me on the slick surface, and I fell face-first. My three front teeth were the first to hit the floor, and they came out—roots and all. In fact, they were actually stuck in the gym floor! Someone ran for the school nurse, and she pulled my teeth from the floor. Somewhere she had read that if you put teeth back in quickly after an injury like that, they might reattach. So, the nurse and I ran down the street to the dentist's office, with the nurse holding my three front teeth in the palm of her hand. The front of my shirt was covered in blood.

When we walked into the dentist's office, we unexpectedly found my mom sitting in the lobby, ready for her long-scheduled routine cleaning. She took one look at me and screamed! The dentist said, "No, you can't shove the teeth back in and hope they'll take root." So, there I was, in eighth grade, missing my three front teeth. The dentist said he could replace my missing teeth with dental implants, but he also pointed out that I could get them knocked out again. From that point on, I always wore a plate, which I removed when I practiced or played. It seemed to bother other people a little bit, but it never bothered me.

My eighth-grade year coincided with the 1960 presidential election between Richard Nixon and John F. Kennedy. One day, during social studies class, our teacher asked us which candidate we supported. I had a crush on one of my classmates, Kathy McCullough, who was Catholic. "Who's for John Kennedy?" the teacher asked, prompting a show of hands. I didn't know much about politics—I couldn't tell a Republican from a Democrat—but I knew that Kennedy was Catholic, and I wanted to impress Kathy. So, in a class of about thirty students, I was one of only three who raised their hand. That gesture sparked a friendship. In fact, she and her parents invited me to join them for a campaign event in nearby Wheaton, where John Kennedy was making a stop. (Coincidentally, I also saw Nixon as he drove through Batavia campaigning in an open convertible, though he didn't stop.) Kathy became eligible for a driver's license almost a year before I did, so when she got hers, we went on a few dates, and I rode shotgun. She and I have kept in touch over the years and still text each other on our birthdays.

When basketball season rolled around, I got more playing time, mostly because one of my teammates, Wayne Nelson, broke his leg. I was still a liability to our eighth-grade team, though. One of my friends during that time was Kenny Anderson, a year behind me, who later became the star quarterback of the Cincinnati Bengals. The backyard of his family's house bordered ours, so from junior high on, we were seemingly always on a basketball court or a baseball diamond. Early on, Kenny was a better basketball player than he was a football player.

Another friend from that time was Craig Sager, who became a sports reporter for TNT and TBS, and was known for his wild-colored outfits. He and my brother, Greg, were the same age and inseparable, which sometimes got them into trouble. One of the first copying machines in Batavia was at the city library. Craig and Greg came up with what they thought was a brilliant idea. They took a dollar bill to the library and made ten black-and-white copies of the front of the bill (for just 5 cents per copy!), then used scissors to cut out the ten "dollar bills." They then went to a nearby laundromat, inserted a "dollar" into the change machine, and received four quarters for each dollar.

They believed they were the smartest guys in the world and decided to celebrate at the local malt shop. Craig and Greg were chowing down on hamburgers and malts when the cops pulled up. The man who ran the laundromat suspected something was off and alerted the police. The officers scared the wits out of Sager and my brother, told them that counterfeiting was a federal crime, and took them to the police station. Each of them had to call their parents, and my dad was the first to arrive. He told the cops, "This had to be Sager's idea because Greg's never been to the library." Their punishment was to wash bicycles at the police station on Saturday mornings from nine to noon that whole summer for any kid in town who wanted their bike cleaned.

When I started classes at Batavia High School in 1962, I had reached a height of five feet, eleven inches, though I was still just an average basketball player. The school had four teams: a freshman team, a fresh-sophomore team made up of sophomores and the most talented freshmen, junior varsity, and varsity. I played on the freshman team and switched my jersey number from 24 to 44 in honor of my friend and former classmate John Cory. John had moved with his family at the end of eighth grade to nearby Maple Park, Illinois, where he attended Kaneland High School, a rival of Batavia High. Coincidentally, when John arrived at Kaneland, he chose 24 as his jersey number! I wore number 44 for my entire basketball career, except during my first season with the Nuggets, when my teammate Ralph Simpson already had that number, so I wore number 25 instead.

On weekends during the summer after my freshman year, I worked in food prep at Twin Elms, a popular local restaurant that served only a few items: a hamburger, a cheeseburger, a pork barbecue sandwich, a beef barbecue sandwich, and curly fries. It was a small, hole-in-the-wall spot, but people would line up on weekends to place carryout orders. My job mainly involved prepping curly fries. One weekend, I stayed home to work at the restaurant while the rest of my family went up to our rustic cabin on Turtle Lake in Wisconsin, where we sometimes got away to relax. Dad wanted to do some painting there, so he took the old Rambler

Ernie Banks of the Chicago Cubs was my sports hero. From Little League through high school, I wore his iconic number 14 every time I played baseball. (Courtesy National Baseball Hall of Fame and Museum, Cooperstown, N.Y.)

station wagon he used for work and left the Pontiac Bonneville, our family car, at home.

After work that Saturday, I decided to drive the Pontiac to visit John Cory at his new house in Maple Park. I wasn't old enough to have a driver's license, but having grown up on the farm, I knew how to drive. Part of the trip was on a gravel road, and when I pulled into John's driveway, he came out and mentioned that I had a headlight out. I figured a stone from the gravel road had probably kicked up and broken it. So, we went to a gas station to get it fixed, and it ended up costing me my entire paycheck from Twin Elms to replace the headlight on the Pontiac!

I took John home, then went back to the house and parked the car in the garage. I thought I had gotten away with my joyride, but about two days later Dad came into my bedroom and asked, "Who replaced the headlight in the car?" I had no idea it was already out, so I was busted. He wasn't too mad, but he said, "Don't ever do that again." Looking back, though, it was kind of his fault. If he'd left the Rambler at home instead of the Pontiac, I never would have taken it to John's!

I didn't have the skills to make the sophomore basketball team, but by the start of my junior year two things changed my athletic path: I grew to six feet, seven inches, and Batavia High School hired Don Vandersnick as the new varsity basketball coach. But that almost didn't happen.

During the summer between my sophomore and junior year, the Batavia School Board met to discuss the vacancy for head varsity basketball coach, along with other school matters. My dad—who was a board member—attended along with his good friend Butch Yeager and George Kramer, who was the chief of police at the time. All three of them were huge fans of Batavia High School basketball and knew there was some real talent coming up through the program.

One of the items discussed was the newly hired school librarian, who had been brought in from Iowa. Apparently, her husband had been a junior high basketball coach there. Some board members who weren't particularly interested in athletics suggested that, in order to save money, they should just hire him as Batavia High's new varsity basketball coach. That way, they'd only have to pay for one move.

During a break in the meeting, Butch turned to my dad and George and said, "I don't like the way this discussion is going." Then he added, "When we go back in there, I'm going to fake a heart attack. We've got to stop this."

So, they went back into the meeting, and sure enough Butch pretended to have a heart attack, effectively ending the meeting then and there.

Later on, the board narrowed the coaching candidates down to two: Don Vandersnick and Duncan Reid, who was an assistant coach at Pekin High School, which had a very successful basketball program. But when they interviewed Coach Reid, he said he didn't want his players participating in any other sports; he wanted them to focus solely on basketball. The board didn't like that. Being a small high school, Batavia needed athletes to play multiple sports just to field full teams. That's ultimately why Vandersnick was offered the job.

Coach Vandersnick saw potential in me that no one else did, and under his guidance I became a decent player. My teammates and I nicknamed him "Vince" because he not only favored former Green Bay Packers coach Vince Lombardi's style but also enforced the rules just as strictly. I've always said there's two ways to motivate people: one is to pat them on the back, and the other is to kick them in the tail. I seemed to respond best to a kick in the tail, and most of my coaches were like that throughout my career. Coach Vandersnick was a taskmaster. He had the varsity basketball players come in before school started. We took our shirts off, put tennis shoes on, and shot free throws. After school, we'd practice for about two hours, and then he'd keep me for an extra half hour or so. We worked on footwork in the low post, dribbling to the basket from the perimeter, and fifteen-foot jump shots. Thank goodness the extra work paid off, because it required a significant commitment.

Coach Vandersnick had a three o'clock curfew on game days, so if we had a game on a Saturday night, we had to be off our feet and home by that time. One Saturday, a few of us on the team were playing cards at the house of one of our cheerleaders, and it was getting close to three. I had driven there with Kenny Anderson, a sophomore. I turned to him and said, "Okay, it's time to go." Some of the other guys protested, saying, "Coach Van won't check. Let's stay and play a little longer." I replied, "No. Kenny and I are leaving." Coach Van did stop by the house, and as a result the guys who stayed and played cards longer were benched for the first half of the game that night. That was the first game Kenny started as a sophomore, and because of that I've always felt a sense of responsibility for his first start on the basketball team. I also started to realize that I might be able to play a bigger role in the history of Batavia basketball than I had so far.

2

Turning Point

Coach Van had a lot of talent to work with in his first year as our head coach. We had three returning senior starters: forwards Gerry Sytar and Larry Heidelberg and guard Tom Skea. The other two starting spots were filled by me at center and fellow junior guard Dean Anderson, who was the best overall athlete at Batavia High. He was the guy in our class that everybody admired and looked up to. Dean made the varsity baseball and basketball teams as a sophomore, was the starting quarterback over Kenny Anderson (no relation) as a senior, and could shoot in the seventies on the golf course—an all-around outstanding athlete. In fact, during our senior year he was voted "Most Athletic" in the yearbook. He was also well-respected in the Batavia community, so I figured I'd like to earn some of that respect, too.

As a junior, I stood six feet, seven inches tall and averaged around nineteen points per game. Most of my points came in the paint, but I also had a smooth jumper from the free-throw line. So, if we posted up Heidelberg or Sytar and they were being guarded by a smaller opponent, I'd move to the free-throw line for an open shot. That season was a turning point for me. I learned from veteran players and received personal instruction from Coach Van, which boosted my self-confidence, especially since I had been considered a late bloomer.

Our team's collective confidence grew, too, which set the stage for an unforgettable season. Our 1964–65 team hit a streak of play that set

Anticipating a miss from my teammate Kenny Anderson (22), who takes a shot in the post before a standing-room-only crowd at Batavia High.

us apart from every other team in the Little Seven Conference. We went undefeated in conference play and won fourteen games in a row en route to the Little Seven Conference championship, where we defeated the defending champion Sycamore Spartans, 75–61, on their home court.[1] When you're winning every night and dominating teams, your confidence grows fast. It was an ideal environment to develop my skills. It was also special to have the support of the Batavia community, as high school athletics were the heart of the city's social life. When we started winning that season, our gym—which held about two thousand people—was packed every night; you had to arrive early just to get a seat. For a city of only seventy-five hundred, that shows you how important basketball was. The fan support was unbelievable, especially for such a small town.

By the end of regular-season play, articles about the Batavia Bulldogs in the *Chicago Tribune* characterized us as underdogs in the sense of David versus Goliath.[2] Back then, Illinois had 750 high school teams, and competition for the annual basketball championship in Champaign was open to all classifications. Smaller schools like Batavia High, which had fewer than six hundred students when I attended, were usually eliminated in the district tournament. But if you won the district, you'd advance to a regional, then a sectional, a super-sectional, and finally the state tournament.

We began our postseason journey by knocking off the Lemont Indians, 72–60, in the Geneva District tournament. Larry Heidelberg and I combined for forty-nine of our team's points in that game. We went on to beat the Oswego Panthers 72–51 in the Geneva District title game.

In the regional tournament, we defeated the Marmion Military Cadets in the Aurora East regional final on March 5, 1965, which marked our twenty-third win in a row. When our team bus returned from Aurora, we were greeted by more than three hundred fans at Batavia High, many of whom were honking the horns of their cars.[3]

In the first round of the Hinsdale sectional tournament, we beat Elgin 72–64. I scored thirty-four points—twelve in the third quarter—and pulled down twenty-four rebounds.[4] Two nights later we fell to East Leyden, 77–74, in the championship game of the Hinsdale sectional, a contest that went to overtime.[5] Gerry led all scorers in that game with twenty-seven points. I picked up three fouls in the first quarter and fouled out in overtime. My mom and dad were sitting in the stands about three or four rows from the court with my Uncle Floyd Meyer, my mom's brother, and his wife, Phyllis. Uncle Floyd was the only "athlete" in our family; he'd played a little basketball in high school and while in the Navy. After I picked up my third foul, the referee was running down the side of the court when Uncle Floyd threw his coat to protest the call, and the coat landed squarely on the official's head! Nobody would rat him out, though.

After the game, the principal of Batavia, Max Wisner, was holding on to Uncle Floyd's coat. My dad went up to Principal Wisner to retrieve it. Wisner asked, "Is this your coat?" Dad replied, "No, but I know who it belongs to." Wisner said, "Well, I'm going to have to talk to him." Dad shot back, "Max, just give me the damn coat." And that was the end of that discussion!

My uncle had the best shot of the night. He landed that coat right on top of the official's head. No one can say my family didn't support me!

The loss to East Leyden brought our season to a close with a 28–2 record. It had been a long time since a district team had reached the state championship, so we were all very disappointed. One bright spot, however, was that Dean and I still had another year left. Maybe we could make it happen as seniors. In the meantime, most of my teammates and I transitioned to baseball, with plans to try out for the team. I played first base, the same position my childhood hero Ernie Banks played during the second half of his career. I even wore his number, 14. We had a good pitcher in our class, Byron Von Hoff. He was spectacular. It wasn't uncommon for at least a dozen Major League Baseball scouts to attend our baseball games to watch Byron. The New York Mets selected him as the first pick in the second round of the 1966 amateur baseball draft.

That spring I started receiving recruitment letters from college basketball programs. They were sent directly to Batavia High, and someone from the school office would bring them to one of my classes. The first one I got was from the University of Wisconsin, but it felt a bit unprofessional. It included a letter expressing their interest in me as a basketball player, along with a form to fill out—my height, weight, school activities—and a self-addressed stamped envelope to return it. Still, every time I received a recruitment letter, I couldn't help but feel a mix of excitement and disbelief. By the end of high school, I had received about 130 of them.

While college recruitment letters were coming in, the summer gave me a chance to focus on other things, like working with my dad and finding ways to fill my free time. I earned money painting houses with Dad, though I don't think he ever let me pick up a paintbrush. Instead, I did all the grunt work, like sanding and taping. In my free time, I'd shoot hoops on the outdoor basketball court at home. And I'm still not sure what my parents were thinking when they let me buy a Honda 305 motorcycle, which I rode around that summer without a helmet. Looking back, I'm lucky I didn't get hurt. My other vehicle was a 1960 Ford Galaxie convertible, which my parents gave me when I got my license. It was probably smarter to stick to four wheels.

By the time my senior year of high school began, I had grown another inch, bringing my height to six feet, eight inches. I decided not to try out for the football team because it became clear I had a real shot at earning a college basketball scholarship. There didn't seem to be any sense in risking an injury. However, I did join the cross-country team. While I didn't win any ribbons, it was a great way to get in shape for the upcoming basketball season. I even remember then–University of Kentucky assistant basketball coach Joe B. Hall coming to watch one of our cross-country practices.

As basketball season approached, I focused entirely on the hardwood, confident that the conditioning from cross-country would help me hit the ground running. When practices started, Coach Van was just as rigorous with us as he had been the previous year. The workouts were grueling; he expected a lot from each of us. The real pressure, though, came from high expectations for another strong season, especially with Dean Anderson and me returning as co-captains. The other three starters were juniors: Kenny Anderson at guard, Dennis Graves at forward, and Mike Brown at center. I played more of a power forward role. Dennis and Mike were both African American. The sports teams at Batavia High were integrated, and most of the basketball teams we faced were as well.

One of the recruitment letters I received was from Adolph Rupp, who sent me a mimeographed letter dated October 15, 1965. I still have it. The tone of the letter struck me as somewhat egotistical. It read: "Because of the winning tradition and the rugged schedule we play each year, we face a tremendous challenge in every game. To meet this challenge, we must recruit from among the top athletes in the country every year. This means that your play will be carefully analyzed, and that the candidates for the limited number of grant aid we award each year will be screened many times before the season ends." I interpreted this as, "We'll keep evaluating you, and if you continue to meet our criteria, we'll keep recruiting you. If not, best of luck." In the letter, Rupp went on to highlight how many All-Americans and professional basketball players had started their careers

Eyeing a rebound while flanked by two opponents, both focused on the ball.

at UK. "This reflects the caliber of players we recruit here," he wrote. "We hope that you take pride in yourself and that you are among the candidates for future Kentucky teams. Best wishes to you and your team for the coming season." Back then, recruiting wasn't like today, where scouts start tracking players in junior high. It was more a matter of waiting until the end of your junior year for the attention to come. And then, it did.

College scouts began attending our games, and even though I was only six feet, eight inches tall, the announcer at our home games would sometimes add a few extra inches to my height, depending on how many scouts were there. In one particular game, with eight or ten college scouts in attendance, the announcer introduced me as six feet, eleven inches—even though I was nowhere near that tall. He just wanted to make sure the scouts knew I was tall enough to play college basketball!

As the season progressed and more scouts showed up, the buzz around our team intensified while my parents grew apart, at least in the bleachers. At some point they decided they couldn't sit together anymore. Dad was always quiet during the games, while Mom was more animated—jumping to her feet, screaming at the referees. I don't remember if it was the same at away games, but at home games Dad would sit on one side of the gym, and Mom would sit on the other. Just like everyone else in Batavia, they were really into high school basketball.

We finished the regular season with just two losses: one to Marmion and one to York High School in Elmhurst. Everyone seemed excited to see how the Bulldogs would perform in the state tournament. I ended the regular season as the leading scorer in the Little Seven Conference, with 347 points in fourteen league games, averaging 24.7 points per game.

Our postseason path began by winning the district semifinal against Plainfield, 84–55, on February 24, 1966. I scored twenty-four points, and Dennis Graves added twenty-three. The following night, we captured the district crown against Oswego, 43–30, a victory that marked our fifteenth in a row. Next, our team advanced to the Aurora West regional, where we won the semifinals against the Marmion Cadets handily, 94–62, on March 2, 1966. The Cadets—who had defeated us earlier in the season—had a highly recruited prospect who played center, Mike Gyovai. He wound up going to Army and playing for Bob Knight. So, it was a pleasant surprise that we won that game so easily.

Our next game, against Naperville in the Aurora West regional final, wasn't easy, but it ended up being my favorite high school game I ever played. Coach Van's son, Brick—who, honestly, had the worst name for a basketball coach's kid—was about eight or nine years old. He had his own little uniform, and he would dribble out with us, leading us out of the locker room. He'd dribble to the free-throw line and take a shot before we started our layup lines. In a way, he was like our mascot.

With two seconds left in the game, we were down 58–57. Coach Van called a timeout and drew up a play, while Brick had already retreated to the locker room, crying. When play resumed, Dean took the ball out of bounds in front of the scorer's table, nearly at half-court. I set up on the low post on the opposite side from Dean. Tom Stephano, a junior who played as our sixth man, came across the lane and set a pick on my defender. I rolled to the low post on Dean's side, and with one hand he threw a perfect pass toward the basket. I caught the ball and laid it in as the buzzer went off, winning the game by a single point, 59–58.[6] The crowd went wild. Many of our fans rushed onto the floor. We ran into the locker room, jumping and screaming, and Brick couldn't believe what was going on.

Celebrating our narrow victory against Naperville in the Aurora West regional final of the Illinois high school championship during my senior year. That's Coach Van in the back row, next to the shorter Assistant Coach Bob Abbott.

The following week, our opponent in the Aurora East sectional was Proviso East, a school with about twenty-five hundred students at the time. Almost every player on their team could dunk, so during our pregame warmups we slowed down our layup line to watch them. They were doing windmill dunks and other highlight-reel moves. Proviso jumped out to an 8–2 lead, but Coach Van called a timeout and set up a full-court press. Our opponents could run, jump, and dunk, but they struggled with ball handling. We scored thirteen straight points and kept the pressure on for the rest of the game. They got rattled, and once we took the lead, the game was pretty much over. We won 84–69. I scored twenty-nine points—fifteen in the second half—and Dean Anderson added twenty.

With a spot in the state Sweet Sixteen tournament on the line, we tipped off against Wheaton Central in the Aurora East sectional finals on March 11, 1966. Our opponents jumped out to a quick 9–0 lead and never looked back. We managed to pull within seven points three times during

That's me just after releasing the ball against Proviso East in the Aurora East sectional. They jumped out to a big lead early, but once we turned up the pressure with a full-court press, they started to unravel. We won the game 84-69.

the game, but we could never get any closer.[7] In the end, we lost 93–81. I scored twenty-one points, and my co-captain, Dean Anderson, added eighteen. It was hard to go to the locker room after that game, knowing that our prep careers were over. I remember taking the bus back to Batavia High. When we arrived, the gym was packed with people even though it was late in the day. We went up on stage, and Coach Van introduced each of us. It felt like the entire town came out to support us. Being a part of that was truly special, as it marked a significant moment in Batavia basketball and remains one of the most memorable experiences of my life.

I decided not to play baseball or compete in track that spring, to focus on college recruitment visits. I also chose to skip school to attend the Cubs' opening day at Wrigley Field with Dean Anderson and two of our high school classmates, John Freedlund and Jim Malnar. The problem was, we got caught. We were sitting in the first row of the upper deck when a foul ball came down right in front of us. We all stood up to see where it landed below, and we ended up on WGN's television broadcast

This photograph of me appeared in our church newsletter. For some reason, during my senior year Batavia High decided we'd wear even-numbered jerseys for home games and odd-numbered ones for away games. I might be smiling in this picture, but I wasn't too happy. I wasn't wearing my number 44.

of the game. Someone called the principal's office, named all four of us, and asked, "Why aren't Dan, Dean, Jim, and John in school today?"

On the way home, we stopped at one of the three stoplights in downtown Batavia. One of our classmates was walking down the sidewalk and said, "You guys got caught!" We knew we were in trouble, so we confessed to our parents. All our parents had to write excuses, but Dean's mom took it to another level. Her note read, "Please excuse Dean from school yesterday because he went to Wrigley Field to welcome home the Cubs." Now that's parental support!

Speaking of parents, Mom and Dad accompanied me on my first college recruitment visit, which was to Northwestern. I think my parents were attracted to the fact that a four-year scholarship to Northwestern was valued at around $12,000 at the time. They also really liked Larry Glass, who was the head basketball coach there. As for me, I was more interested in going to Wisconsin. Neither school had a particularly strong basketball program, but I really liked Madison. My friends back in Batavia would say, "You don't want to go to Northwestern. That's where all the rich kids from Chicago go, and the girls wear mink coats to the fraternity parties. You won't fit in at all."

Our visit to Northwestern coincided with the Waa-Mu Show, an original musical written, performed, and produced by Northwestern students each year. It's on par with productions you'd see on Broadway. Coach Glass and his wife invited us to attend the show, and afterward my parents went to dinner with them while I went out with one of the current Northwestern players and his girlfriend. We went to a burger joint and ordered hamburgers with French fries. To my surprise, my hosts ate their burgers with a knife and fork. That's when the alarm went off in my head, based on the advice from my buddies: "*You don't belong at Northwestern!*" So, I like to joke that I chose Kentucky because at least the basketball players there eat their hamburgers with their hands. I should mention that Pat Scanlon, my speech class teacher at Batavia High, had just recently graduated from Northwestern. When she heard that Northwestern was recruiting me, she said, "With your work ethic and academics, you'd be at Northwestern for about six weeks." Her words hit me hard, and I suddenly realized just how high the bar really was. I began to doubt whether I'd be able to keep up and make the grades—no matter which college I chose to attend.

Another school I visited as a recruit was the University of Wisconsin. At the time, the NCAA had the National Letter of Intent, and some conferences also required their own "conference commitment letters." As a senior, I signed a nonbinding conference commitment letter to attend Wisconsin, but I never signed the National Letter of Intent. John Erickson was the coach at Wisconsin back then, and he even came to my high school graduation. I also made official recruiting visits to the University of Iowa and the University of Michigan. I had never seriously considered the University of Illinois, but one day the program's then–assistant coach, Howie Braun, asked to come by our house in Batavia to make a recruitment pitch. He was bringing along one of his players, Bill Small, who had gone to West Aurora High School, just down the road from us.

Before I sat down at the dining room table with my parents, Coach Braun pulled a thick, business-sized envelope from his pocket and slapped it down on the table. He never mentioned what was inside. Instead of talking up the Illinois program, he spent the next twenty minutes criticizing Northwestern and Wisconsin—the schools I was considering at the time. Finally, my dad said, "Well, Coach, we really appreciate you coming, but Dan has no interest in going to the University of Illinois." Coach Braun reached out and grabbed the envelope—presumably filled with cash, though he never said a word about it—and slipped it back into his pocket. He was visibly upset, and my dad had to literally escort him out the front door, with Bill Small and my mom following behind. Bill even apologized to my mom on the way out. Until the day he died, my dad often joked that his one big regret was not opening that envelope before he showed Coach Braun the door!

My final visit as a recruit was to the University of Kentucky. I flew into Louisville, my first time ever on an airplane. Coach Hall and Phil Argento, one of the Wildcat guards, picked me up at the airport and drove me to Lexington. I stayed in the dorm with Phil and some of the other players. Besides touring the campus, I visited two Thoroughbred breeding and training farms: Calumet and Elmendorf, which no longer exists. Due to my background, I found the experience fascinating. It sparked a love for horses and horse racing that I still have.

In addition to exploring the campus and learning about Kentucky's horse racing history, I had the chance to meet Coach Rupp for about twenty minutes in his office at Memorial Coliseum. I still remember the instructions Coach Hall gave me before I went in to meet him. Coach Hall said, "He'll say something you think is funny, but if he doesn't laugh, don't you laugh. He might also say something you don't find funny at all, but if he laughs, you laugh along with him." It felt like I was about to meet the Pope in person! I don't recall details of our conversation, but Coach Rupp had more pictures of Hereford cows on the walls of his office than anything related to basketball. As a kid who grew up on a farm, that stuck with me.

While I was on the UK campus, I came across a story about basketball recruiting in the *Kentucky Kernel* school newspaper. The article listed at least fifteen prep players that Coach Rupp was recruiting, organized by position. Among them were guards Mike Casey and Mike Pratt. The top choice center mentioned was George Janky from St. Rita High School in Chicago, followed by Joe Bergman from St. Mary's High School in Iowa. I turned the page, expecting to see my name listed third, but that was the end of the article. My name wasn't mentioned at all. I left Lexington feeling like I wasn't really wanted. Soon after, Janky signed with the University of Dayton and Bergman committed to the University of Iowa. That's when Kentucky's recruitment of me really picked up. In fact, Coach Hall came to Batavia and stayed for three or four days, accompanying my dad as he painted houses. One afternoon, around five o'clock, Coach Hall called our house while I was home and asked if he could stop by to talk. I told him, "Well, I've got a date at seven o'clock, but if you want to come over now, feel free." So, I sat in the kitchen with Coach Hall, Mom, and Dad. When 6:45 p.m. rolled around, I thanked him for coming, then got up and left. When I got home around 11 p.m., my dad had already gone to bed, but Coach Hall was still sitting at the kitchen table, talking with my mom!

My dad and I then took a second recruiting trip to Kentucky, and this time they were much more aggressive. We flew into Blue Grass Field in Lexington. As the workers positioned a mobile stairway for our exit, someone unrolled a long, red carpet. The flight attendants looked around, wondering who the carpet was for, and were surprised it was for a fresh-faced seventeen-year-old kid. Inside the airport terminal, Coach Rupp, Hall, and fellow assistant coach Harry Lancaster greeted us and arranged for us to stay at the Imperial House Motel, which was one of the nicest motels in town at the time.

Dad had never been to the UK campus, so we toured it together. During our visit we also met Armand "Mondo" Angelucci, a UK graduate and Lexington attorney who would become a close friend. He helped my dad—and me—get a sense of how I would be treated and just how special it was to be a basketball player in Lexington. Mondo took us to dinner and hosted us at his home, where we met his wife, Joyce, and their two young boys.

A day or so later, just before we were about to head to the airport to return home, we were in our hotel room with my dad, Coach Rupp, Lancaster, and Mondo. Coaches Rupp and Lancaster pushed me to sign right then and there, but Dad stepped in and said, "No. You give us the offer sheet, and we'll take it home. If Dan decides to come, we'll sign it and send it back to you."

When we got home, I remember Dad coming into my bedroom and saying, "If you're really serious about this basketball thing, Kentucky has had more All-Americans and professional players than any other school in the country." I was surprised because this was the first time either he or Mom had mentioned any school other than Northwestern. So, I signed the offer sheet and sent it back. I was a Wildcat.

3

From Kitten to Cat

In August of 1966 my parents drove me from Batavia to my new home in Lexington: the old Haggin Hall, which was a bit run-down. My assigned roommate was Mike Pratt, and although we didn't hit it off right away, we eventually became great friends. We weren't the best match as roommates because our personalities clashed. Mike, a city boy, was extroverted and confident, while I was from a small town and more introverted. About a month into the school year, we agreed to switch roommates. Mike had bonded with Mike Casey, and that turned into a lifelong friendship, so he moved in with him on another floor of Haggin Hall. Randy Pool, a forward from Oak Ridge, Tennessee, moved in with me and stayed my roommate for the rest of my freshman year.

As we settled into our new living arrangements, I quickly found that the talent on our freshman basketball team, known as the Kittens, was even more impressive than I had imagined. The roster included Casey, who was named Mr. Basketball in Kentucky, and Pratt, who earned the same honor in Ohio. We also had Randy Pool, the best player from Tennessee; Travis Butler, the best player from Alabama; and several players from the Kentucky All-Star roster: Casey from Shelbyville, Bill Busey from Bagdad, Jim Dinwiddie from Leitchfield, Terry Mills from Barbourville, and Clint Wheeler and Benny Spears from Ashland.

Memorial Coliseum was packed for the freshman games, often before the varsity game even started. And in scrimmages, while we were called the

Kittens, we gave the upperclassmen Cats all they could handle. Outside of those matchups, though, we didn't interact much with the varsity players. Then-senior Pat Riley seemed to want nothing to do with us, but his classmate and All-American Louie Dampier kind of took me under his wing. In fact, during Coach Hall's grueling preseason conditioning program, which focused on running, Louie turned to me and said, "Stick with me." Part of the program involved doing sprints every Monday, Wednesday, and Friday, gradually increasing until we were doing twelve 220-yard dashes a day. And they all had to be completed in under thirty seconds. Refusing to push himself more than he needed to, Louie perfected the art of getting his foot across the finish line just as the stopwatch hit thirty, so I modeled my approach after his.

While our freshman team was gaining attention for its talent and energy, we were also adjusting to the demanding structure of life at Kentucky. Harry Lancaster was the freshman coach and ran practices with the intensity of a stern Marine sergeant. This was a contrast to his friendly demeanor when he was recruiting me. During one practice, Bill Busey was dribbling the basketball while Coach Lancaster was speaking. Lancaster turned around and barked, "Don't dribble that ball while I'm talking!" A little later in the practice, Coach stopped everything to make a point—and there was Bill, dribbling the ball again. "Busey," Lancaster said, "if you dribble that ball one more time while I'm talking, I'm going to nail your ass in a coffin and ship you back to Bagdad." So, it was a big adjustment going from being recruited to playing at Kentucky.

But the adjustments didn't end with basketball. Off the court, I was equally challenged, especially when it came to academics. I was terrified about getting good grades because I had been an underachiever in high school. So, I spent a lot of time studying and didn't do much socially. I don't remember missing a single class. By midterm of our first semester, only a few of us freshman basketball players had grades above a 2.0. You needed at least a 2.0 to play, and the team trainer, Spike Kerns, was supposed to be our academic advisor. One day we gathered in a small room in Memorial Coliseum, and Coach Rupp chewed us out about our poor academic performance. Then this guy walked in wearing a trench coat. His name was Claude Vaughan, an economics professor. After my playing career, Coach Rupp told me, "I figured it'd be easier to teach an economics professor how to tape ankles than to teach a trainer how to be an academic advisor."

The Kentucky brain trust: Coach Rupp (left) and Coach Lancaster, arguably the greatest head coach and assistant coach duo in college basketball history. (Courtesy of the *Lexington Herald-Leader*, photograph by E. Martin Jessee.)

The intervention didn't stop with that meeting. From that point on, any of my teammates with a GPA under 2.0 had to attend a study hall run by Claude for a couple hours every day. I'd taken Pat Scanlon's warning to heart, so thankfully I was spared having to attend. Somehow, I managed to get a 3.75 my first semester and a 3.50 my second semester.

All of these adjustments started to wear on me at times. In fact, there were moments during my freshman year when I nearly quit because I was so homesick. Aside from one week at the Ray Meyer Basketball Camp in northern Wisconsin during the summer between my junior and senior years of high school, I had never been away from home. I never spoke about my homesickness to my teammates or the basketball coaches, but I did confide in Mondo Angelucci, who became a great friend and mentor. Every Sunday afternoon, I would go over to the Angeluccis' house in Lexington to watch sports on their television and have dinner with Mondo, Joyce, and their two boys. It was the family atmosphere I was missing in the dorm. During those visits, I would sometimes say, "It sure would be nice to be with my family." Mondo and Joyce helped me get through those bouts of homesickness—not just with their advice, but with their love and the comfort of their home. I would also go over every Tuesday night to watch *The Fugitive,* a popular television show. It became something special we shared.

While I may have doubted myself at times, it became clear that the UK coaching staff was happy with their decision to recruit me. In a handwritten note to my parents dated October 17, 1966, Coach Hall wrote that I looked "tremendous in the fundamental practices that we have had so far. If he continues to work like he has this week he will have a great future. He is even better than I had hoped." My parents never mentioned this letter.

Kentucky's varsity team struggled during the 1966–67 season, finishing with a 13–13 record and an 8–10 mark in SEC play, which only fueled the buzz around our freshman squad. We ended the season with a solid 18–2 record. One road trip that stands out took place in mid-January, when we flew to Huntington, West Virginia, on a Sunday morning to play the Marshall University freshmen that night. To say the basketball staff and athletic department were frugal would be an understatement. Instead of booking hotel rooms for the afternoon, we were taken to the home of Joe Holland, a former Wildcat basketball forward who had played from 1945 to 1948. We spent the afternoon in his living room watching Super Bowl I between the Green Bay Packers and the Kansas City Chiefs. That night, we defeated Marshall 120–105.

Outside of basketball and academics, my best friend that year was Steve Cody, who lived across from me in Haggin Hall. Steve was from Naranja, Florida, and had never seen snow before. He was free-spirited, and we often found ourselves making late-night trips to a Waffle House near the UK Medical Center that stayed open all night. I'd walk in, order breakfast, and sit at one end of the counter. Steve would come in about five minutes later and sit at the other end. We wouldn't acknowledge each other.

The Waffle House had a small staff, and the same person would take your order, cook your food, and serve it. So, I'd distract the cook by paying my bill while Steve would take off running for the door. Since the cooks changed frequently, we were able to get away with this every two or three weeks. I always paid for my meal, but Steve would never pay his bill. He'd just dash out before anyone noticed. Looking back, it wasn't a smart thing to do. Steve was lucky he didn't get caught. I didn't think it would be good for a basketball player to be arrested for a misdemeanor.

While we were getting away with pranks like that at the Waffle House, I decided to try something a bit more respectable: fraternity life. With

Eager Kentucky fans watch warm-ups.

a few exceptions, nearly all of the basketball players joined one of two fraternities: Pi Kappa Alpha (Pike) or Sigma Alpha Epsilon (SAE). Louie was a Pike, so Pratt, Casey, and I decided to pledge to the Pikes. After our first pledge meeting, three or four of us were assigned to wash and dry all the dishes from the fraternity dinner that night. Growing up, Greg, Kathi, and I had to split dishwashing duties at home, and I absolutely hated it. I'm not sure why, but I couldn't stand it. That night at the Pike house, though, I didn't complain. I washed and dried every dish with the other pledges, but when I left, I told myself I wasn't coming back. A few days later, some of the Pike members asked why I hadn't returned. I explained that while pledging was part of the fraternity experience, it just wasn't for me. So, they made me a social member, which meant I could attend all the parties and become friends with the chapter members. Steve Cody eventually became my little brother in Pike.

That spring, horseman and Kentucky basketball booster Tom Gentry (I called him Tommy) took me to Keeneland for the first time, and I was hooked. After the first race, let's say the number 2 horse won—he pulled a $10 winning ticket on number 2 out of his pocket and handed it to me. Then, after the second race, the number 7 horse won. And sure enough, he handed me another $10 ticket—this time on number 7. What I didn't realize at the time was that Tommy had a $10 winning ticket on every horse in each race. He just had to remember which pants pocket it was in!

Occasionally we would have lunch in the dining room at the Keeneland Club, and he had a box that was right on the finish line. After we were done with lunch, we would go to the box and watch the races.

While Tommy was perhaps best known as being one of the first people to buy older mares and make a profit selling their offspring, he was also a natural salesman. If you attend a sale at Keeneland today, you'll find identification and promotional materials attached to the horse stalls that help buyers and visitors identify them. Tommy started all of that. I remember one time, later during my time at UK, we had gone to the races at the former River Downs in Cincinnati. On the way home, we stopped at The Maisonette, which was a five-star restaurant. In those days, they still had ashtrays on the tables. And they had Tommy's name—Tom Gentry—engraved on one of the matchbooks by the ashtray.

Tommy, always thinking ahead, called the maître d' over and asked, "How do you do this?" The maître d' replied, "Well, we've got a little machine. You set the type, and then you emboss the matchbooks." That gave

Tommy an idea. He decided to create custom matchbooks for potential buyers attending future Keeneland horse sales. These were wealthy individuals, but they thought receiving a matchbook with their own name on it was the greatest thing that had ever happened. Tommy's racing colors were blue and gold, so when he designed the matchbook covers, he had the names of friends or prospective buyers embossed in gold print. He was always thinking about how to promote himself and his horses.

For many years Tommy hosted a big party at his horse farm to coincide with Keeneland's July horse sale. Tommy's party was the social event of the year in Lexington, and being invited was a real thrill and honor. He booked top-tier entertainment, like Bob Hope and The 5th Dimension. One year he had a circus theme, complete with elephant rides and helicopter rides. He did not bear any cost for this party. If you had ten horses in the sale and owned even a fraction of one, your share of the party expense—however small—came out of your proceeds.

Some people didn't like Tommy's style of self-promotion. But my dad told me a long time ago not to judge people by what other people say about them. You judge people by how they treat you, and Tommy always treated me terrifically.

But that was years later. Back in my freshman year, I was still figuring out who I was and what kind of person I wanted to become. After finals in the spring semester, I returned to Batavia to work for a company that built prefabricated homes. I earned good money and spent time with my friends that summer, all while looking forward to my sophomore year at UK. I played plenty of pickup games with Greg, Kenny Anderson, and other friends at the basketball hoop in the driveway of my parents' house. As much as I enjoyed being back with my friends and family, I began to realize that we had different agendas and goals. For the first time, I understood what people mean when they say you can't go home again. So, when I returned to Lexington for my sophomore year, the homesickness was gone.

As the summer ended and I returned to Lexington, I realized that Coach Rupp's approach would be a far cry from what I had experienced as a freshman. That fall, every practice began with a half hour of shooting. We were instructed not to talk or socialize with our teammates. Instead, we were expected to shoot, chase the rebound, dribble back out, and shoot again. This routine helped me develop an outside jump shot, which served me well throughout the rest of my career. We received good instruction,

It feels like I'm shooting down at the basket in this one.

and I believe I became a better rebounder and defensive player at UK. But more than anything, Coach Rupp and Coach Lancaster instilled in me the importance of a strong work ethic. I had a solid work ethic before I arrived at Kentucky, but they pushed me to refine it even further. They didn't allow any shortcuts. If you came in and didn't meet expectations, they might forget your name, especially if they thought you were wasting one of their scholarships. But if they saw you were contributing to the program, they stayed on you.

During practice, Coaches Rupp and Lancaster wore starched khakis and pressed shirts, which gave the impression of military officers running the show. Sometimes Rupp quoted lines from Theodore Roosevelt's famous speech known as "The Man in the Arena." Part of it reads: *It is not the critic who counts; not the man who points out how the strong man stumbles, or where the doer of deeds could have done them better. The credit belongs to the man who is actually in the arena, whose face is marred by dust and sweat and blood, who strives valiantly; who errs and comes short again and again; because there is not effort without error and shortcomings; but who does actually strive to do the deed; who knows the great enthusiasm, the great devotion, who spends himself in a worthy cause, who at the best knows in the end the triumph of high achievement and who at the worst, if he fails, at least he fails while daring greatly. So that his place shall never be with those cold and timid souls who know neither victory nor defeat.*[1] That summed up Rupp's philosophy perfectly, and I identified with it. In fact, to this day I still carry those typewritten words on a tattered piece of paper in my wallet.

Coach Rupp was known for his superstitions. During his time as head coach at Freeport High School in Rockford, Illinois, he wore the same brown suit for every game until it became worn and tattered. Over his four years at Freeport, Rupp compiled an impressive record of 59–22, including a third-place finish in the 1929 Illinois high school state tournament. From that point on, he continued to wear his brown suit on the sidelines, earning the nickname "the man in the brown suit."

Another superstition Rupp had was that he would only use the same urinal in the locker room. And woe to anyone who happened to be using it when he entered. Coach would not tolerate anyone else occupying "his" spot. Rupp also believed that finding a hairpin before entering an arena brought good luck. For road games, our trainer and academic adviser, Claude Vaughan, would be among the first off the bus. He'd scatter three or four bobby pins on the sidewalk, ensuring that Coach Rupp could find one before heading inside.

When regular-season play began, Casey, Pratt, and I were in the starting lineup, but it took us some time to find our rhythm. About halfway through the season, on January 15, 1968, we hosted the Georgia Bulldogs. I was sidelined for most of the first half due to foul trouble. Then, with

I considered the one-point win against Tennessee on February 12, 1968, at home to be our greatest victory of the year. Just a month earlier, the Volunteers had blown us out by twenty-eight points. The postgame crowd shot says it all. (Courtesy of the *Lexington Herald-Leader*, photograph by E. Martin Jessee.)

about fifteen minutes left in the second half, I was undercut while going up for a layup, landing on my head and suffering a severe concussion.[2] I was told I walked off the court, but I don't remember anything until I woke up at the UK Medical Center. They had transported me there by ambulance. I didn't score in that game, which marked the only time I went scoreless during my UK career. Two games later, we lost to the University of Tennessee, which had a really strong team, falling 87–59—one of Rupp's worst losses as a coach. That was the low point of our season. But about a month later we edged Tennessee by one point at home, 60–59.

When we were on the road, we'd always have a pregame meal in the early afternoon, and then I'd usually go for a walk by myself to collect my thoughts. We were at Ole Miss on February 6, 1968, and I went for a walk in Oxford, Mississippi. Like many old Southern communities, there was a courthouse in the middle of the town square. In front of the courthouse, there were two drinking fountains—one with a sign that read "White" and the other with a sign that read "Colored." In 1968, seeing two separate water fountains like that was unbelievable to me, because I grew up in the North and had played on integrated teams my whole life. It made me think

That's my college sweetheart, Cheri (top left), a member of the cheerleading squad at old Stoll Field on the UK campus.

about a contemporary of mine: Perry Wallace, the first African American basketball player in the SEC to compete in a varsity game. The verbal abuse he endured playing in the South just because of his skin color was outright criminal. It didn't make sense to me, given my own background.

All season long, I had my eye on an attractive blonde named Cheri Hughes, a cheerleader for the Wildcats and a graduate of Lafayette High School in Lexington. I asked her out several times but kept striking out. One of the male cheerleaders, Tom Sweet, who lived across the hall from me in the dorm, told me Cheri was dating her high school sweetheart. Still, I wasn't ready to give up. During a road trip to Athens, Georgia, on February 19, we beat the Georgia Bulldogs 106–87 to capture the SEC championship, securing our spot in the NCAA tournament and finishing the regular season with a 21–4 record and 15–3 in SEC play. The cheerleading squad had flown in on their own plane. After we cut down the nets and headed to the locker room, Tom Sweet cornered me and said, "Cheri needs a ride home when we get back to the airport. If you want to give her a ride, you can." The cheerleaders would take an earlier flight back to Lexington, but Tom assured me Cheri would be waiting for me when our plane landed. I jumped at the chance. There was a crack in the door, and I wasn't going to miss it.

When our plane touched down at Blue Grass Field, around two thousand fans were there to celebrate the win. The cheerleaders' plane had already arrived. As I walked down the steps, a UK student I'd casually dated a couple of times rushed up, threw her arms around me, and kissed me on the cheek. I was a little taken aback and thought, *Oh, okay!*

Cheri, who was in the crowd, witnessed the whole thing. I quickly told the girl I needed to grab my bag from the other side of the plane, then ran into the terminal. Inside, I spotted Cheri heading toward a phone booth to call her dad for a ride. I stopped her, explained that I didn't know the girl (even though I did!), and said I still wanted to give her a ride home. She reluctantly agreed, but she still didn't believe I didn't know the girl who'd kissed me on the cheek.

Except for one semester when she was pledging for her sorority, Cheri lived at home with her parents, Mary and Virgil Hughes, while attending college. So, that was our destination. When I pulled into their driveway, I asked if we could go out sometime. I wanted to make a date right then and there, but Cheri hesitated and said she wasn't sure. A few nights later, she called and said, "I'm at the library. If you want to come pick me up, we can do something." When I picked her up, we went to a drive-in movie. She didn't want to be seen in public with me! And that was the start of our relationship.

In the first round of the NCAA Mideast Regional Tournament, held on our home court, we faced the Marquette Warriors (now known as the Golden Eagles). This game stands out to me because their coach, Al McGuire, didn't get along with Rupp. In fact, Rupp had invited McGuire, along with the other two coaches in the regional tournament—Fred Taylor of Ohio State and Madison Brooks of East Tennessee—to be guests on his weekly television show. However, McGuire never showed up. He did, however, make a statement to the press intended to intimidate, claiming that Warriors center Pat Smith was "psyched" to get the center jump on me, even though he was five inches shorter.[3] That really motivated me.

When the game tipped off, I won the jump ball, and we went on to beat the Warriors handily, 107–89. I had one of the best games of my career, scoring thirty-six points and grabbing thirteen rebounds. Casey

Mike Casey (34), Mike Pratt (22), and I were known as the "Super Sophs." Here we are with Coach Rupp on media day at the start of our junior year. (Courtesy of UK Athletics.)

scored nineteen points and Pratt added eighteen. During the postgame press conference, a reporter asked Rupp if McGuire's comments had fired me up. "Yes," Rupp said. "In fact, they fired the whole team up."

The next night, we suffered a heartbreaking loss to Ohio State, 82–81, in the Mideast championship game. With just three seconds left on the clock, their forward, Dave Sorenson, hit a turnaround jumper from about six feet away to seal the win.[4] We were devastated, especially after how well we had played against Marquette. Casey, Pratt, and I truly believed we had a shot at making the Final Four in our first year of varsity basketball, but that's the way it goes sometimes. We finished the season with a 22–5 record.

I didn't have much time to dwell on the loss, though. Mike Casey and I were invited to try out for the 1968 U.S. Olympic basketball team in Albuquerque, New Mexico, in early April. Coach Rupp told us to ask our professors for permission to miss a month of classes. Once we arrived in Albuquerque, eighty-eight athletes competed for a spot on the roster, including players from the NCAA, the AAU, the Armed Forces, the NAIA, and junior colleges. The head coach was Hank Iba of Oklahoma State. Some of the nation's top Black players, including Elvin Hayes and Lew Alcindor, who changed his name to Kareem Abdul-Jabbar, declined invitations to try out in protest of the treatment of Blacks in the United States. In a 2017 interview with NBC, Abdul-Jabbar explained his decision, saying he wanted to "point out to the world the futility of winning the gold medal for this country and then coming back to live under oppression."[5]

After one of our tryouts, Casey, Pete Maravich of LSU, Rick Mount of Purdue, and I went to a drive-in, where we had a drink or two. Close to midnight, we left the drive-in to find a place to eat and stumbled upon a bowling alley in Albuquerque with a packed parking lot. Once inside, we ordered hamburgers and fries and watched the bowlers. The place must have had twenty to twenty-five lanes, and every one of them was in use. Then, out of nowhere, Pete left our group and walked to the far end of the alley. Without warning, he started skipping across the lanes as people were bowling! He ran by us and said, "If you're going with me, you better come on!" So, we ran out of the bowling alley and headed back to the hotel. No harm, no foul. Before Pete found Jesus later in life, he was a live wire.

Among the NCAA players who made the final roster were Jo Jo White from the University of Kansas, Charlie Scott from the University of North Carolina, Bill Hosket from Ohio State, and Ken Spain from the University of Houston. Believe it or not, Maravich didn't make the cut. I was selected as the first of six alternate players.

Before formal competition began, the team was scheduled to head overseas for a three-week tour to play exhibition games, but Jo Jo White and Bill Hosket stayed behind to finish their academic semesters. This opened up two spots on the tour—one for me and one for Tom Black, a center for the old Akron Wingfoots, an Amateur Athletic Union team sponsored by the Goodyear Tire Company, who had been chosen as the second alternate. This meant a trip to the U.S. Military Academy for a week of workouts before the overseas tour began. But before leaving for West Point, I attended my first Kentucky Derby. At the time, Cheri volunteered for Angel Flight, a women's organization that supported the Air Force Reserve Officers' Training Corp (ROTC). There was a designated area in the Churchill Downs infield reserved for Angel Flight members, so I went with Cheri. I knew the Derby was a big deal, but I had no idea just how massive the crowd would be. Standing in the infield, I looked over at the clubhouse and grandstand, and every seat was filled. The place was packed, and it was overwhelming. I was hooked. I remember pointing to the clubhouse and telling Cheri, "I'm never coming back until I sit in one of those seats."

Dancer's Image won the race that day, but a few days later he was disqualified after traces of phenylbutazone were found in his post-race urinalysis. As a result, Forward Pass was declared the official winner. That year, then–presidential candidate Richard Nixon attended the Derby, and Cheri, along with the other Angel Flight members, lined up across the track to form a path for him to walk through on his way to the winner's circle. (The following year, I attended the Derby with my friend Tom Gentry, and we sat in one of the clubhouse boxes. I began going to Keeneland more often since it was much closer to campus. I couldn't make it for the fall meet due to commitments with the basketball preconditioning program and the start of formal practices, but by the time the spring meet rolled around in April, there weren't many days I missed.)

Soon after the unforgettable experience at the Derby with Cheri, my journey with the U.S. Olympic basketball team took me to Europe for the first time, where the sights, sounds, and culture were a world apart from what I'd left behind in Kentucky. Stops on the tour included visits to Yugoslavia, Russia, Finland, and Norway. As an alternate, I didn't get much playing time, but one unique experience was visiting Red Square in Moscow. One of our stops was the mausoleum where Lenin's body was preserved in a glass case—pretty creepy, honestly. People lined up for blocks just to view him lying in the tomb. We were given rubles to buy souvenirs, but I spent most of mine on long-distance phone calls to Cheri back in Lexington. One of our team's forwards, Mike Silliman, was from Louisville and had played for Bobby Knight at West Point. He tipped me off to a marketplace in Moscow where they sold Oriental rugs and advised me to buy a three-by-five-foot rug as a keepsake. I paid $100 for it and stuffed it in my suitcase. Since then, I've tried to get it appraised, but it has no label. That rug still sits in the foyer of my home to this day.

When I returned to Lexington after the tour, I was three credits short of being eligible to play basketball my junior year. To make up the difference, I had to take a correspondence course in Kentucky geography. I passed the test with ease, but looking back, I can't help but wonder what would have happened if I hadn't passed that course!

That summer, I stayed in Lexington and worked as a grade checker for the Carey-Adams Construction Company, which developed many subdivisions in the area. My role involved ensuring the land or project site was prepared to the correct elevation and slope according to the design plans. I'd place spikes in the ground, measure the road level relative to those spikes, and then instruct the earthmover operator to add or remove material—usually by two inches—depending on the situation.

One day, about halfway through the summer, two of the earthmover operators failed to show up for work. The project foreman wasn't happy because we were on a tight deadline to finish that subdivision. I was one of three or four grade checkers on site when the foreman asked, "Does anyone here know how to drive a tractor?" I raised my hand and told him I had learned to drive a tractor when I was about twelve. He then showed me how to operate the earthmover, including how to raise and lower the blade to hit the grade. After making three or four passes with me to help me get the hang of it, he said, "It's all yours."

As a result, I got a nice raise and spent the rest of the summer driving that massive earthmover. Cheri and I were going strong, and I was looking forward to a promising junior year with the Wildcats. Life was good.

4

First Steps Toward Forever

During our junior year, Cheri and I began to spend a lot of time at the Red Mile harness racing track in Lexington. We had a circle of friends we often saw there, including Harry and Pat Miller. Harry was a prominent attorney in Lexington and very much in Coach Rupp's inner circle. He and Pat were part of a small group—maybe four or five couples—who would travel with us on road trips or gather for dinners.

One evening Harry and Pat hosted us for dinner at their home. Harry had grilled a roast and left it on the table while he and Pat were wrapping up the rest of the meal. They had a big standard poodle who decided to help himself to the main course. He jumped up on the table and grabbed the roast. Pat managed to wrestle it away and placed it back on the plate like nothing had happened. Cheri witnessed the incident, unbeknownst to Pat. She quietly told me, and when I noticed a tooth mark in the slice on my plate, I carefully cut around it.

Harry was also president of the Red Mile, so whenever we went, we had a good seat, either at Harry's table or up in the box. That's where I first got to know Gib Clowe, a harness horse trainer and driver. We hit it off, and that's how I came to later own my first racehorse. More on that later.

My life was changing in more ways than just horse racing. I had attended church all my life, but never outside of the Lutheran denomination until I met Cheri. Her home church was Broadway Christian Church in Lexington, which was pastored by Marshall Leggett, so I began attending services there every Sunday. When I told my parents, they were supportive. They were just glad I was still going to church! Mom believed that she had attended church only if communion was served. Broadway Christian was traditional and served communion every Sunday. They also had an organist for the music, not a band, so I think that was fine with Mom.

My relationship with my faith grew and changed as the years went on. It wasn't a case of turning to the Lord because there was nowhere else to go; that wasn't my story. What drew me to Broadway Christian was the fact that it had great music, a good message, and I could attend with Cheri. That was the most important part. In fact, Pastor Leggett would later say that even if I had a game on Saturday night, I'd still be in church early Sunday morning. I never had the heart to tell him that it was probably more about Cheri than it was about Jesus!

As I continued to grow in my faith, I began to see the deeper truth that life is full of both highs and lows, and in all of it God's faithfulness remains constant. God is always with us. I'm reminded of the story of Job in the Bible. Job had everything: thousands of donkeys, camels, and sheep, and a large family that he deeply loved. But one day, Satan came before the Lord, and the Lord said, "Have you considered my servant Job? You may test him, but spare his life." Soon after, thieves stole all his livestock, and the building where his family was gathered collapsed, taking the lives of all his sons and daughters. Job's body was covered in painful sores and boils. He was truly brought to the lowest point.

Even his wife urged him, "Curse God and die." But Job replied, "The Lord gives, and the Lord takes away. Blessed be the name of the Lord." This is a powerful lesson for us. One of the great promises we have is that God will never take us where His grace can't sustain us. Another promise is that God loves us—He wants to bless us and work through us. All we need is the faith to believe in that promise. Yet, too often, we become consumed with the day-to-day worries and challenges, focusing more on the problems than the promises.

As Christians, we should focus on the promises we have in Christ. One of my favorite Bible passages is Philippians 4:4–5: "Rejoice in the Lord always. I will say it again: Rejoice! Let your gentleness be evident to all. The Lord is near."[1] I love these verses because they present a message that stands in contrast to the worldview that life is a dog-eat-dog struggle, that we have to be tough and hide our weaknesses. But Paul encourages the Philippians to "let your gentleness be evident to all." This passage doesn't

Cheri and I barely acknowledged each other during games.

promise that faith will shield us from financial hardship, illness, or life's challenges. But it does assure us that if we bring our burdens to the Lord, He will give us a peace that "surpasses all understanding," a peace that no one else can figure out.

As we face the struggles of life, we're reminded of the importance of trusting in God's peace and guidance, even when things seem uncertain. That's how I felt as I faced a personal challenge of my own—one that required not just courage but also faith. Before the grind of another basketball season began, I decided to ask Cheri to marry me. But, wanting to do things the old-fashioned way, I asked her father for permission first. Cheri's dad, Virgil, loved to fish, so I took him on a lantern fishing trip to Herrington Lake, just south of Lexington. We stayed out all night with a lantern hanging over the side of the boat. The problem was, I never could muster up the courage to ask him. As the sun started coming up, we headed back to the dock. I was freezing, wearing three pairs of pants just to stay warm. My fingers had gone numb, so I had to ask Virgil to unzip my pants so I could go to the bathroom before we headed back to Lexington.

On the forty-minute drive back, I was still too nervous to ask. But just a mile from their house, I finally got the courage. I turned to Virgil and said, "Would it be alright if I asked Cheri to marry me?" He shrugged and replied, "Yeah, I guess that would be all right." And that was the end of the conversation. Virgil used to joke that not only did he lose a daughter that day, but he also lost a fishing partner, because I never went fishing with him again!

With that task behind me, I proposed to Cheri on Thanksgiving Eve. There was a parking lot on the UK campus, near the baseball field, the practice football field, and not far from the dorm complex where I lived. I had a fraternity pin, which you give to your girlfriend as a symbolic gesture—more serious than "going steady," but not quite an engagement. Earlier that year, in that same parking lot, I had given Cheri my pin. So, to continue the tradition, that's where I took her to propose. We were in my car when I popped the question. I think she had been expecting it; she was all in. Happy Thanksgiving indeed!

I knew the next step was to tell Coach Rupp. It felt a little like asking Virgil for Cheri's hand—I was nervous. I walked into his office, and I can remember the conversation like it was yesterday. I said, "Coach, I just wanted to let you know that I'm getting married this summer." Coach Rupp replied, "Do you have to?"

I said, "No, sir. I don't have to."

He responded, "We haven't had anybody here get married who didn't have to since Billy Ray Lickert in 1958." He went on, "When you get married, basketball doesn't come first anymore."

I replied, "Well, Coach, with this girl, basketball hasn't come first for a while," a remark I'm sure he didn't find amusing. He said, "Well,

I can't stop you. There's nothing I can do about it, but I certainly don't agree with it."

A few days after my talk with Coach Rupp, our basketball season tipped off with a dominant 115–77 victory over Xavier at Memorial Coliseum. Expectations were high, as Casey, Pratt, and I brought a lot of on-court experience from the previous season. Phil Argento was our only senior, and we also had a solid group of sophomores, including Larry Steele, who was making an impact on the team.

A week later, we suffered an 87–77 loss to North Carolina at home, but quickly bounced back, winning the UK Invitational Tournament with a 112–104 victory over Michigan and an 80–65 triumph over the Army Black Knights. Army was coached by Bob Knight and led by their point guard, Mike Krzyzewski.

The game I remember most from the early part of that season was our matchup against Wisconsin on New Year's Eve at Chicago Stadium. At the time, we were ranked third in the country, and Wisconsin—the school I had once considered attending—was one of the worst teams in the Big Ten that year. A bunch of my family and friends from Batavia came in on buses to watch the game, and Cheri and her family drove up from Lexington to be there too.

I played horrendously, probably the worst game of my junior year. I scored twenty-two points on nine for twenty-one shooting. Pratt added fifteen and Argento chipped in fourteen, but it wasn't enough.[2] Wisconsin won, 69–65. It was a huge upset, and I can still remember walking into the locker room after the game. Coach Rupp went off on a rant. He came right up to me and said, "We scheduled this game for you. We scheduled it so all your people from Batavia could come to watch you play. We scheduled it against Wisconsin because that's where you were thinking about going. And all you did was shit in my hat and pull it down over my ears!"

Then he started yelling at Casey and Pratt for a while, before turning back to me. "And YOU! You shit in my hat and pulled it down over my ears!"

By the third time he said it, I couldn't help but picture exactly what he was describing, and I had to bite my tongue to keep from laughing. In a way, it gave me a bit of comic relief after such a terrible game.

I think the pressure of having so many family members and friends from Batavia there may have affected my performance. Some nights just don't go your way, and unfortunately that was one of those nights. But after that fiasco in Chicago, we went on to win eleven straight games. We finished the regular season as SEC champions, with a 16–2 record in conference play.

Our first opponent in the Mideast Regional was Marquette, in Madison, Wisconsin, on March 13, 1969. One of our student managers, Doug Billips, had entered the Marquette locker room before the game to grab ice or something, and he overheard Al McGuire's pregame speech. According to the manager, McGuire seemed to frame the game as a black-versus-white contest, especially since our team had no Black players. And with Marquette being so close to Milwaukee, the crowd was naturally biased in their favor. The Warriors got the best of us that day. We shot just 40.6 percent from the field, four of our five starters fouled out, and we lost 81–74.[3] I scored only thirteen points. I think Coach Rupp was starting to realize that his coaching prime was coming to an end. His health wasn't great, and he desperately wanted to win one more championship before retiring.

But beyond the pressure of the game, playing at Kentucky meant living under constant scrutiny. Your life was always under a microscope, and not everyone was rooting for you to succeed. If players misbehaved in public, some people were quick to call Coach Rupp and rat us out. I remember one time after a game, Mike Casey and his family, along with my parents and me, went out for dinner. Casey's dad, Dutch, and my dad ordered a pitcher of beer. Casey and I weren't yet twenty-one, so we didn't drink. The next day, we were called into Coach Rupp's office. He said, "I heard you boys were having a beer last night." I told him, "No, Coach, that was my dad and Casey's dad drinking, but we didn't have a drop. You can call my dad and ask him." Someone at the restaurant had seen the pitcher of beer on our table and couldn't wait to report us.

There was a place in Versailles called Wilson's Pool Room, where Casey, Pratt, and I would go. Nobody bothered us there. No one turned us in. That was our spot whenever the three of us went out together.

That summer, I planned to operate the earthmover for Carey-Adams Construction again, but Pratt and I were invited to meet with Dan Stafford, president of Daniel Boone Fried Chicken, a chain with three locations in Lexington and one in Georgetown. Entertainer Sammy Davis Jr. was on the board of directors, and former Kentucky governor A. B. "Happy" Chandler was chairman of the board of Commonwealth Security Investors (CSI), an investment company that merged with Daniel Boone

Fried Chicken in May 1969. Stafford offered to hire us for the summer to drive the company limousine, transporting Chandler from his home in Versailles to the company's Lexington headquarters each weekday. We'd also pick up visiting board members at Blue Grass Field when they flew in.

I told Stafford I was getting married that summer and was counting on the $150 per week I'd make working for Carey-Adams. To my and Mike's surprise, he crunched some numbers with an assistant and offered us a salary of $200 per week! It was a cushy job for two college kids. We drove that limo around and had lunch almost every day for free at one of the restaurant locations. But the easy job ended abruptly. In late July, a group of New York–based bankers acquired the company,[4] and Pratt and I met with the new CEO.

"I see you boys are making quite a bit of money, but we can't figure out what you do," he said. "The warehouse out back needs cleaning up. We'll pay you $2 an hour to clean it out." Mike and I looked at each other, then told him, "No, I think that'll be all." With only a couple of weeks left in the summer, it wasn't a huge loss. In hindsight, I'm glad we walked away. About a year later, the Securities and Exchange Commission filed a lawsuit against CSI and the previous owners of Daniel Boone Fried Chicken, including Dan Stafford and Happy Chandler, accusing them of falsifying records and other federal crimes.[5] The company went under, and the case was settled out of court.

Without a doubt, the highlight of that summer for me was marrying Cheri. One of the best pieces of advice we received came from Pastor Leggett during our premarital counseling. He told us, "Get your faith together." At the time, I was still a member of the Lutheran church. He said it didn't matter whether we were Lutheran or part of the Christian church. What mattered was that we shared our faith journey.

The wedding ceremony and reception were held at Broadway Christian, with Pastor Leggett officiating. My brother, Greg, served as best man, and Cheri's sister, Vicki, was the maid of honor. I also had five groomsmen: Casey, Pratt, Steve Cody, and two high school friends, John Freedlund and John Malnar. The reception took place in the church basement, where punch and wedding cake were served—no booze. Coach Rupp and his wife attended, and they gave us the most thoughtful wedding gift: a sterling silver tea set and tray. I'm sure that was Mrs. Rupp's idea; Coach Rupp himself was known to be frugal.

Cheri and I were married on June 14, 1969, at Broadway Christian Church in Lexington—a very happy day. Pictured here with our parents.

After the reception, Cheri and I left for Louisville, where we spent the night at the Executive Inn before driving to Gatlinburg, Tennessee, for a three-day honeymoon. Meanwhile, my dad hosted an open bar party at the Downtowner Motor Hotel and Restaurant on Main Street in Lexington for out-of-town guests and Cheri's family. Dad told me that when they opened the bar, Cheri's family was practically knocking each other out of the way to get to it! He got a real kick out of that.

As much as we were celebrating, the summer was also shadowed by some hard news. The low point came when we learned that Mike Casey had been in a serious car accident. He hit a light pole on the driver's side and suffered a compound fracture of his left leg. At first, we didn't fully grasp how severe the injury was, but by the time our senior year began, we learned that he would miss the entire season. Casey was our leading scorer during the 1967–68 sophomore season and became our second-leading scorer as a junior. He wasn't the fastest player on the court, but he was exceptional. Mike had a natural ability to anticipate where the ball was

The 1969–70 Wildcats. *Back row, from left:* Me, Art Laib, and Mark Soderberg. *Middle row, from left:* Doug Billups (manager), Clint Wheeler, Larry Steele, Mike Pratt, Tom Parker, and Claude Vaughan (trainer and academic advisor). *Front row, from left:* Adolph Rupp, Stan Key, Kent Hollenbeck, Jim Dinwiddie, Terry Mills, and Joe B. Hall. (Courtesy of the University of Kentucky Libraries Special Collections Research Center.)

going. Whether he was shooting, rebounding, passing, or scoring, he excelled in every aspect of the game.

When classes started at UK in the fall of 1969, Cheri and I were beginning our final year of college as newlyweds, doing our best to stretch every dollar. Because I had a basketball scholarship, I was allowed to go through the food line at the student center. They didn't itemize the bill; they just sent it to the athletic department. As long as things didn't get too out of hand, no one said anything. Cheri and I would go for breakfast and share one tray between us. After classes, we'd meet again for lunch and do the same thing. For dinner, we'd usually go to her parents' house or to a booster's place. We didn't have much money, but we didn't know we were missing anything. We were just happy to be together.

As basketball season got under way, my daily routine began to center more around the team. We entered the season ranked as the number one

Pulling down a rebound against the North Carolina Tar Heels on December 8, 1969. (Courtesy of Jay Leviton Archives.)

team in the country, despite the loss of Casey. We only lost two games that year, but I couldn't help but think that, with Casey, we might have made a serious run for the championship. Pratt and I talked about that often.

The loss of Casey opened up more opportunities for our guards, particularly Jim Dinwiddie, Terry Mills, and Stan Key. However, those were some big shoes to fill. The most satisfying win of my senior year came on December 8, 1969, when we finally beat North Carolina, 94–87, at Charlotte Coliseum, prior to the start of SEC play. We had lost to UNC in each of the previous two seasons, and they had a formidable lineup. Charlie Scott, a senior and All-American, led the team, along with a talented sophomore forward, Bill Chamberlain.

The only loss of the regular season came at Vanderbilt on January 31, 1970. For some reason, we just didn't play well there. I had a bruised heel and wasn't at 100 percent, though I'm not sure how much that affected the outcome. I do remember playing the game on the tip of my right foot, trying to manage the pain.

One of my dad's goals was to visit every SEC school during my career, and he was able to check off another one when he attended our matchup against Ole Miss in Oxford, Mississippi, on February 7, 1970. Cheri flew

Acknowledging the crowd near the end of our last home game in Memorial Coliseum during my senior year. (Courtesy of the *Lexington Herald-Leader,* photograph by E. Martin Jessee.)

in with some boosters. We won the game handily, 120–85,[6] and I scored fifty-three points, setting a new individual game record for the UK men's basketball program. At the time, the record was fifty-one, held by Cliff Hagan since 1953. I also broke Cotton Nash's career scoring record earlier in the game. (Cotton ended his career in 1964 with 1,770 points in seventy-eight games. I finished my career scoring 2,138 points in eighty-three games.) Having Dad and Cheri there to witness those milestones made it even more special.

After the game, Coach Rupp came up to congratulate me. He said, "I don't know how I feel about you breaking Cliff's record," referring to Hagan, who was one of his favorite players. Then he added, "But I sure am glad you broke Cotton Nash's career scoring record." The story goes that Cotton was the only player who could talk back to Coach Rupp and get away with it, because he was such a dominant player on those teams, and Rupp didn't have the option to reprimand him.

When Jodie Meeks broke my single-game scoring record by pouring in fifty-four points against Tennessee in 2009, I was working for a water

Game action during our 109–99 win against Notre Dame in the Mideast Regional semifinals. (Courtesy of the *Lexington Herald-Leader*, photograph by Frank Anderson.)

company I owned, and Cheri and I were in a hotel in Wyoming watching the game on the television. At halftime, I told Cheri, "Jodie's gonna break my record," and sure enough, he did. The next morning, I called him to congratulate him. He's a great guy.

The NCAA Mideast Regional took place in Columbus, Ohio, on March 12, where we faced off against the Notre Dame Fighting Irish. Their roster included All-American guard Austin Carr, who would go on to play for the Cleveland Cavaliers. For the first five minutes of the game, I barely touched the basketball, which prompted Coach Rupp to call a timeout. In the huddle, he said, "I want to introduce you to Dan Issel. He's the all-time leading scorer at the University of Kentucky. Now get him the damn basketball!"

We got into some foul trouble during that game but managed to pull out a 109–99 victory. I finished with forty-four points, Pratt added fourteen, Terry Mills scored thirteen, and Tom Parker chipped in twelve.

Two days later, we faced off against the Jacksonville University Dolphins, a formidable opponent led by their seven-foot-two All-American center, Artis Gilmore. Like us, the Dolphins had only one loss going into postseason play—a narrow 89–83 defeat to Florida State and their star center, Dave Cowens. For some reason, our coaching staff showed us film from that particular game, which I never quite understood.

Leaving the arena in Columbus with Cheri after our Mideast Regional semifinal victory over Notre Dame. At right, that's Cawood Ledford in the hat behind Coach Rupp. (Courtesy of the *Lexington Herald-Leader*, photograph by Frank Anderson.)

In addition to Gilmore, Jacksonville had two other towering players: seven-foot Pembrook Burrows and six-foot-ten Rod McIntyre. They also had a strong backcourt.

We got into serious foul trouble during that game. I fouled out with ten minutes and thirty-two seconds remaining. The play that did it came when Dolphins point guard Vaughn Wedeking positioned himself behind me at midcourt while I was running back, with my head turned in the opposite

Reflecting on the end of my Wildcat career in the locker room after our loss to Jacksonville University. (Courtesy of the *Lexington Herald-Leader,* photograph by Frank Anderson.)

direction. So, the last ten minutes of my college career were spent sitting on the bench, watching the game unfold. Pratt fouled out next, followed by Mills and Steele.[7] Despite the foul trouble, our teammates stepped up and played well. We lost by just six points. I always reminded Artis Gilmore that I only played twenty-nine minutes yet still managed to score twenty-eight points. Parker added twenty-one and Mills had eighteen.

Legendary Ohio State football coach Woody Hayes came into the locker room after the game to speak with Coach Rupp, but I was numb from the loss, trying to process the end of my Wildcat career. It was incredibly disappointing. I mentioned earlier that Coach Rupp was really focused on winning one more championship. He had lost the 1966 NCAA championship to Texas Western, despite being the favorite. I felt terrible for having disappointed him, because he meant so much to me and to our team. I was sad for myself, but I was also sad for him.

That year, I averaged 33.9 points per game. I was fortunate enough to play twenty-five years of organized basketball, and my four years at Kentucky were my favorites by far. My senior year, in particular, stood out. Even though we didn't make it to the Final Four, we had an incredible season, with only one regular-season loss: to Vanderbilt. We were ranked number one in the country before the NCAA tournament. I had just gotten married, was having a great year on the court, and we were winning a lot of games.

I completed the spring semester of my senior year but fell short of the credits required to graduate. Over the next two years, I took some correspondence courses, yet I never finished my bachelor's degree in business, and I regret that. It's one of the few things in life I started but didn't finish.

Despite that personal regret, I was honored to see my accomplishments on the court recognized back home. After my career at Kentucky ended, the city of Batavia put up three signs with a green background and white lettering at three main entrances along the roads leading into town. The signs read: "Batavia: Home of Dan Issel, All-American, 1969–1970." Not long after they went up, two of the signs were stolen. To protect the remaining one, the city took it down and placed it in the lobby of the Batavia National Bank, where it stayed for a while. Today, my son, Scott, has that sign hanging in the workout room of his home.

While it meant a lot to be remembered in my hometown, my attention shifted to the next big step: figuring out where to begin my professional basketball career. As the school year came to a close, that decision consumed much of my focus. During my senior year, I was constantly getting calls from agents. Back then, anyone could represent you; there were no requirements, no need for a law degree, and no approval process. As a result, the industry was full of shysters. I remember hearing about one agent who charged a player 25 percent of his contract just to represent him. It was crazy.

I didn't sign with any agent because I felt I had put in all the hard work to get where I was. I wasn't about to give away 10 or 15 percent of my contract just for someone to negotiate it on my behalf. But after consulting with my dad, I decided to ask Mondo to represent me in any contract negotiations. We trusted him implicitly. Toward the end of the year, I received a call from former UK standout guard Cliff Hagan, who was serving as player-coach for the Dallas Chaparrals in the ABA, a team that would eventually move to San Antonio and become the Spurs. Cliff told me, "Dan, I'm happy to inform you that the Dallas Chaparrals have your draft rights in the ABA." I replied, "Cliff, I really appreciate that, but there's only one team I'd consider playing for in the ABA, and that's the Kentucky Colonels." And that was the end of that conversation.

About a week later, I received another call, this time from Wendell Cherry, a member of the Colonels' ownership team, informing me that the Kentucky Colonels now held my ABA draft rights. After conferring with Mondo and my dad, I arranged a meeting with the team owners to negotiate a contract with the Colonels before the 1970 NBA Draft took place. I was excited because I loved Kentucky, and it was Cheri's home state. It seemed like an ideal situation. Mondo also suggested we bring Pratt into the meeting, since the team had expressed interest in signing him as well.

The Colonels' ownership group was a Who's Who of business leaders in Louisville. It included Stuart Jay, a prominent lawyer; Wendell Cherry and David Jones, the founders of Humana, a leading health care organization; David Grissom, president of Citizens Fidelity Bank (now PNC); and John Y. Brown, then-owner of Kentucky Fried Chicken. Pratt and I arrived at the meeting accompanied by our fathers, Mondo, and my Uncle Marvin, who worked in the insurance business. We had no intention of signing a contract that night, but as the discussion unfolded, it became clear that an agreement was within reach, until John Y. Brown abruptly stormed out. He wasn't happy with some of the compensation figures being discussed. "I think you're all crazy talking about these numbers," he said.

Despite that, the rest of us hunkered down and eventually signed a deal around one o'clock in the morning. The owners proposed a package deal for both Pratt and me, which we accepted. My share came to less than half a million over the five-year contract period, which was about what I could expect in the NBA—a lot of money for a farm kid. There was also deferred compensation, along with an agreement that the Colonels would pay off the mortgages on both my parents' and Cheri's parents' homes. We were thrilled about that. Pratt's contract was for three years, with the third year being nonguaranteed. Once the deal was finalized, we celebrated by heading to a Waffle House in Louisville for breakfast and sharing a triple chocolate pie. I was a Kentucky Colonel.

5

Life as a Colonel

Before I signed with the Colonels, Cheri and I had rented an apartment in Lexington. Our only furniture was a king-size bed that my parents had given us as a wedding gift, along with a few hand-me-down pieces from Cheri's parents' basement. With some steady income now coming in, about $3,500 per month, we decided to put down roots in Louisville. After touring a Homearama, we chose a two-story, three-bedroom Tudor-style model home in the Green Spring subdivision. It was fully furnished, plastic flowers and all. The move was the easiest we would ever have; just our bed and the clothes from our Lexington apartment, and we were settled! We were excited to begin this new chapter of our lives.

Not long after arriving in Louisville we started to attend Southeast Christian Church, a small congregation pastored by Bob Russell. We eventually became good friends with him and his wife, Judy. At my request, Bob baptized me one Saturday night, with only Cheri, her parents, and my parents there. I had been baptized previously in the Lutheran tradition as a baby through sprinkling, but in the Christian church baptism is done by full immersion.

Bob performed my baptism in fishing waders, but I displaced so much water that the baptismal tank overflowed the top and soaked his pants. Afterward, we were all waiting and wondering where he'd gone. It turns out he was back in his office trying to dry his pants with a hair dryer! Despite the comedy, it was a meaningful moment. We were acting on Marshall

My biggest fans! When possible, my parents wouldn't sit together during my games. They each had their own way of cheering me on. Mom was expressive and fully into it, while Dad was quieter and more subdued.

Leggett's advice to get our faith in order. That night, I officially joined the Christian church. Aside from being a U of L fan, Bob's a pretty good guy.

I wasn't the only All-American college player to sign with the ABA in 1970. Others included Charlie Scott, who joined the Virginia Squires, and Rick Mount, who signed with the Indiana Pacers. Meanwhile, All-Americans who chose to sign with the NBA included Pete Maravich (to the Atlanta Hawks), Calvin Murphy (to the San Diego Rockets), and Bob Lanier (to the Detroit Pistons).

The excitement in Louisville was palpable when the Colonels signed Mike Pratt and me to join our top scorers, Darel Carrier and Louie Dampier, on the court. Then, the ownership group made another big move, hiring Mike Storen away from managing the Indiana Pacers. Storen was widely regarded as the best general manager in the ABA at the time. I didn't have any direct dealings with him when I signed my contract, but he and I arrived around the same time, which was another boost for the organization. For the first time, many people thought the Colonels might become a legitimate franchise with championship potential. Incidentally, Mike's daughter, Hannah Storen—who goes by the professional name Hannah Storm—became a well-known anchor on ESPN SportsCenter. I've known her since she was eight years old.

What always amazed me about Mike was his loyalty. Prior to joining the Colonels, he had drafted and signed Rick Mount to the Pacers. Rick's career just wasn't working out—mainly, I think, because he didn't really have the heart for basketball. But Mike stayed loyal to Rick and even went so far as to bring him to the Colonels by a trade. Mike was also deeply loyal to the ABA. He even served a year as commissioner, and after that he became the general manager of the Memphis Tams, hoping to save the struggling franchise.

Here's a funny story about one of my Colonels teammates, Cincy Powell. A lot of guys back then handled their own contracts, and Cincy used to say you could always tell when Mike wasn't being completely honest. Cincy was in Mike's office one time, negotiating his contract. He said Mike would look you straight in the eye until he said something that wasn't true. During the negotiation, Mike told him, "Cincy, we just can't afford any more. We're paying you all we can." And right then, Mike's eyes darted off to the corner of the office.

At the start of my rookie year, the coach was Gene Rhodes, who had previously been an assistant basketball coach at Western Kentucky University, where he once played. However, he and Mike Storen didn't see eye to eye, and fifteen games into my rookie season the Colonels fired Gene. None of the players knew it at the time, but in his final game as coach, with only a few seconds left, Gene began walking down the press row, shaking hands with everyone. When the game ended, he walked toward the back of Freedom Hall. He didn't turn toward the locker room—he just kept walking out the back door into the night. Storen had to come into the locker room to inform us that Gene had been relieved of his duties.

Alex Groza, a standout player at Kentucky and our business manager, stepped in to coach two games, both of which we won. That put our record at 12–5. To bring more legitimacy to the organization, the owners hired Frank Ramsey as head coach. Frank was a Hall of Fame player at Kentucky and with the Boston Celtics, where he essentially invented the role of the sixth man. At the time, he was back in his hometown of Madisonville, and the owners persuaded him to come on board as the Colonels' coach.

Right after they hired Frank, Coach Rupp called me. He explained that Frank's father had owned seemingly half of Madisonville, and Frank had bought several other businesses there with money he earned from the Celtics, including a bank, a nursing home, and a lumberyard. Coach Rupp told me, "Frank's having a little cash flow problem right now. He'll be your coach for one year. It doesn't matter if you're great or terrible—he's not staying longer than that."

You often hear coaches described as "player's coaches," and Frank was one of them. He would sit in the locker room and engage in conversations with the players while we were getting dressed. I had other coaches who would stand in the locker room before a game, writing things on the board, but I'd never had a coach pull up a chair and include me in the pregame discussions. I remember one time in Denver, down at the old arena, playing against the Denver Rockets. Frank started a discussion about mutual funds. He was teaching us what mutual funds were, using chalk to illustrate his explanations on the concrete blocks of the wall. Finally, someone knocked on the locker room door and said, "Hey, are you guys going to warm up? It's about ten minutes until game time." Frank was a Kentucky native and a talented coach who was inducted into the Naismith Memorial Basketball Hall of Fame in 1982. At my request, he presented me during my Hall of Fame induction in 1993.

Life as a pro basketball player took some getting used to, as I went from playing two games a week in college to three or four—sometimes even five. We played eighty-four games in the ABA. Of course, I didn't have the responsibility of attending classes and keeping my grades up, but playing for the Colonels felt like an extension of my college days since we were still in Kentucky, still representing the state. In my rookie year, the ABA didn't have many standout centers, but the players were still incredibly talented. I was facing a higher level of competition every night compared to the SEC. There were adjustments to be made, but the best part was getting paid to do what I loved. Without question, my most formidable individual opponent during my rookie season was Mel Daniels, the center for the Indiana Pacers. I hated playing against Mel because not only was he big, but he also had the lateral movement to come out and guard me on the floor. The Pacers were like the early Celtics of the ABA, with their success and the championships they won. At that time, Mel Daniels was by far the best center in the ABA. The rivalry between the Colonels and the Pacers was always the most intense.

Finger roll in an exhibition game against the Baltimore Bullets on September 22, 1971. (Photograph by Mark Gordon.)

On the road, I roomed with Darel Carrier, a veteran who had been with the Colonels for three years. Darel had his favorite restaurants that he would visit, but aside from attending pregame shootarounds or eating out, he mostly stayed in his hotel room. That's when Louie Dampier and I started to hang out. We had known each other since my freshman year at UK, when he was a senior, but we quickly developed a great friendship.

Besides eating out, on off days we'd pass the time by going to a racetrack or catching a movie. Starting with my second season, Louie and I roomed together for the rest of my time with the Colonels. Our per diem was around $12 a day, so we didn't exactly dine at steakhouses. We had to stick to inexpensive places and probably ate more fast food than we should have. The diet we had back then, today's NBA players would just shake their heads at. We consumed a lot of cheeseburgers and fries in those days.

Our 1970–71 regular season under Frank didn't end as hoped. We finished with a 44–40 record, falling below .500 for the games he coached and ending eleven games behind the Virginia Squires, who took first place. The Squires were a formidable team, featuring standout players like Charlie Scott, Doug Moe, George Carter, Neil Johnson, Ray Scott, and Larry Brown. Personally, I was having a strong season, earning second-team All-ABA honors and sharing Rookie of the Year honors with Charlie Scott. I averaged 29.9 points per game, while Charlie averaged 27.1. I also narrowly edged out Rick Barry of the New Jersey Nets for the league scoring title, as Barry finished with 29.4 points per game. I have Frank to thank for that. With our playoff spot secured, Frank made a key decision before the third-to-last game of the season against the Carolina Cougars. "We're going to feed Dan tonight," he told our team. "And we want him to score as many points as possible to win the scoring championship." That night, I scored fifty-one points. In the second-to-last game, we faced the Memphis Pros, a team I had struggled against, so Frank decided to have me sit out. I think it was the only game I missed my rookie year. In the final game of the regular season against the Pittsburgh Condors, I scored fifty-one points again, securing the scoring title over Barry.

In the Eastern Division semifinals, we faced the Miami Floridians and defeated them in game six on their home court, 112–103. In the second round, we were up against the Squires—the team that finished eleven games ahead of us. To the surprise of many, we won game six in Freedom Hall, 129–117, advancing to the ABA Finals to face the Utah Stars, who had the second-best record in the league that year, finishing 57–27, behind only the Indiana Pacers. Utah had a strong roster, including Zelmo Beaty, a former NBA star who had moved to the ABA, along with Willie Wise and Glen Combs, a native of Hazard, Kentucky. They held the home court advantage.

Each home team won their games. We lost the first two in Salt Lake City but bounced back to win the next two in Freedom Hall. We then

This photograph shows the shooting form I learned from Coach Van and Coach Rupp: straight legs, straight arms and elbows, and bent wrists. (Photograph by Mark Gordon.)

lost game five in Utah but won game six at home. Unfortunately, we lost game seven in Salt Lake City, 131–121 on May 18, 1971. Zelmo Beaty and I kind of offset each other in that game. I scored forty-one points, and he had thirty-six. Despite the loss, we certainly exceeded postseason expectations. "I don't see any reason why these guys should hang their heads," Frank Ramsey told reporters after the game. "They did a terrific job—they went farther than anybody anticipated."[1]

During this era of pro sports, many athletes took off-season jobs to supplement their income, as salaries were not in the tens of millions like the contracts for top talent seen today. One of our team owners, David Grissom, hired me that summer to work in the correspondent bank division of Citizens Fidelity Bank, which he owned. I'm not sure if today's banking rules are the same, but back then branch banking didn't exist. Instead, banks operated as standalone entities, and by federal law each bank had to keep 20 percent of its deposits in another bank, known as a correspondent bank. This arrangement was both beneficial and lucrative for larger banks like Citizens Fidelity, as it allowed them to keep their deposits in various locations across the state. My job, along with that of my colleagues Bill Fox and Darrell Thore, was to take bankers out to lunch and dinner. If they were current customers, we worked to keep them happy. If they were customers of other banks, we aimed to persuade them to move their deposits to Citizens Fidelity Bank. We rarely spent the night anywhere; we always made one-day trips so we could return home.

This job really opened my eyes to how important Kentucky basketball is to the entire state. I certainly learned that playing for UK, but this experience made me realize just how deep the passion for the program runs in every corner of the commonwealth, not just in and around Lexington and Louisville. We'd visit small banks in Western Kentucky, and the people there would know all the stats and the names of all the players. For years, the Kentucky basketball program has been a source of pride for the entire state, and that realization cemented itself in my mind. Everywhere we went, people talked about Kentucky basketball, shared their memories of my career there, and marveled at how outstanding the program was. Their pride and admiration for UK basketball left a tremendous impression on me.

By this time, my brother, Greg, had dropped out of college in Missouri and moved to Florida to work for Gib Clowe, the harness horse trainer I'd befriended at the Red Mile. Greg and I became partners in owning

Tom Gentry playfully measures my height with one of his customized yard-sticks—a popular promotional giveaway. Even people with no connection to the horse business would visit Keeneland just to get one.

some of the horses, which was a first for me. There were no cell phones back then, and very few phones at the track. But somehow, if one of our horses won, Gib would find a way to call me within five minutes. If we didn't win, I wouldn't hear a thing.

One day we had a horse who was favored to win. The race came and went. No call from Gib. I figured we didn't hit the board. Then Greg called.

"You know where you finished last night?" he asked.

"No. But I know we didn't win, because Gib didn't call."

"You finished third," he said.

I was surprised. "Oh. I thought we'd do better than that."

"You know what the exacta paid?" he asked.

"No."

"Two hundred and thirty dollars."

"Wow," I said. "Two long shots must've come in ahead of us."

Greg paused for a second, then said, "You know who had the exacta, twice? Gib Clowe." It was a reminder to be careful of who you trust.

That was the day I decided I was done with the harness horse business. Not long after that, I bought my first Thoroughbred mare with Tommy Gentry. I was ready for a new chapter.

Horse ownership wasn't the only thing new I tried that summer. One Saturday morning, I took my first-ever golf outing to Big Spring Country Club with Louie Dampier, my attorney J. Bruce Miller, and a friend of his from the law office. I think someone had just given me a set of clubs, but I'd never had a golf lesson in my life. I could hit worm burners, but I couldn't get the ball in the air.

It didn't help that Bruce was nearly a scratch golfer, and Louie was really good, too. Meanwhile, I was just awful. That one morning, we were on the sixteenth hole, a par 5 that runs up behind the clubhouse and the pool. I told myself, "I'm going to get this ball in the air, no matter what."

I teed it up high—way too high—and took a big swing. The ball shot straight up into the air and came down *boom,* right in the clubhouse parking lot. There must've been seventy-five or eighty cars out there. Louie and I were sharing a cart, and I said, "That sounded like it did some damage. I better go see whose car I hit."

It turned out I hit *my own car,* a Buick Electra. Put a dent right in the trunk. I opened the trunk, threw my clubs in, looked at Louie, and said, "You go ahead and finish. I'll be in the bar."

Game action during an unsanctioned ABA/NBA All-Star game at Nassau Coliseum in 1972. The NBA team won, 106–104.

With my finances in good shape, Cheri and I flew to Hawaii for a month-long honeymoon, extending the three-day trip we had in Gatlinburg. We spent a week on each of four different islands, and Cheri was five months pregnant. We ate constantly, and by the end of the trip we both had to buy muumuus for the flight home. When I showed up at training camp for my second year, I was significantly overweight. I even remember a sportswriter joking that when I weighed in, I must have had my money belt around my waist.

After we lost the championship, our owners signed incoming rookie Artis Gilmore, which was another major move for us. The story goes that the ABA teams would cooperate if they believed one team had a better chance of signing a player than others. They would leave it up to that team to make the acquisition. Supposedly, there was a meeting of all ABA general managers, where each wrote down the amount they would offer to sign Artis. Mike Storen wrote down $3 million on his slip of paper. While he had no intention of paying Artis that amount, it secured us the rights to him, allowing us to sign him away from the NBA.

Meanwhile, Frank Ramsey returned to Madisonville, as Coach Rupp had predicted, so the owners hired Joe Mullaney as our new head coach. Before coming to the Colonels, he had coached the Los Angeles Lakers for two seasons, where he worked with Elgin Baylor, Jerry West, and Wilt Chamberlain. Moving from the NBA and the Lakers to the ABA and the Colonels, I think Joe saw it as a step down, but he quickly realized we had some pretty good talent of our own. One thing I remember is that if someone made a mistake, he'd walk up and down in front of the bench, loud enough for the guys sitting there to hear, and bark, repeatedly, "He's killing me out there tonight!" Joe was an intense guy, that's for sure. We had an incredible season under his leadership, though, finishing with a 68–16 record, which stands as the best in ABA history.

However, we lost to the New York Nets in the first round of the 1972 ABA playoffs, four games to two. We might have been a little overconfident going into that series. What I remember most is that whenever Artis or I touched the ball, the Nets immediately double-teamed us. They also tried to keep the ball out of Louie's hands. Their whole defensive plan was to take me, Artis, and Louie out of the game and force our other teammates to beat them. No one really stepped up, though, even though they were open much of the time. On our side, our defensive strategy was not to double-team Rick Barry but to guard him one-on-one. Rick ended up having a phenomenal playoff series. Those were the biggest reasons we got beat in that playoff matchup.

People might be surprised to learn that during my early playing days I was hooked on soap operas. My favorite one was *Days of Our Lives,* which opened with the iconic line "Like sands through the hourglass, so are the days of our lives."

Postgame interview with Van Vance, the longtime play-by-play radio voice of the Colonels. (Photograph by Mark Gordon.)

I got Louie Dampier hooked on it, too. It became an obsession with us. In fact, whenever we were on the road and checked into a hotel, the first thing we did was grab the printed *TV Guide* magazine to see when *Days of Our Lives* was on. It was just a half-hour show, mostly centered around the trials and tribulations of the Horton family.

One time, our team flew into Salt Lake City for a game, and our arrival coincided with the start of *Days of Our Lives.* The airport had these little chairs, kind of like recliners, where you could pop in a quarter and watch a half hour of television. Salt Lake City's baggage claim was notoriously slow, so we figured we had time. We sat down, popped the quarters in, and watched the whole episode. By the time we made it down to baggage claim, our teammates were gone. The bags had come out, the team had grabbed theirs, and they'd already left for the hotel. Louie and I had to catch a cab, all because we couldn't miss *Days of Our Lives*! After that, whenever we were on the road and missed an episode, we'd call Cheri, and she'd fill us in on everything that happened. But a couple of years later, when the show expanded to an hour, I lost interest and eventually stopped watching.

I had other memorable off-the-court moments as well. One place our team frequented was a restaurant in Louisville called the Normandy Inn. Its owner, Paul O'Brien, was a big sports fan. By the time our games ended, most of the restaurants in Louisville were already closed, but Paul would keep the Normandy Inn open after the games, so many of us would end up there for dinner. Paul was a huge fan of the Colonels, but being from Philadelphia, he considered himself an expert on Philadelphia sports.

One night in January of 1972, we were talking and the name Richie Ashburn came up. He was the center fielder for the Philadelphia Phillies. I said, "Richie ended up playing a year with the Cubs in Chicago." Paul immediately disagreed, saying, "Oh no, he didn't. He played his whole career with the Phillies." I replied, "Paul, not only did he not play his whole career with the Phillies, after the Cubs, he also played a year with the Mets." He insisted, "Oh no." I said, "Alright, let's make a bet." I can't remember what my side of the bet was, but Paul's side was that I could invite three couples to the Normandy Inn, and he'd cover all the food and drinks.

We called the sports editor of the *Courier-Journal*—I think we even woke him up—and asked him to settle the dispute. He had some books on hand, and sure enough Richie Ashburn had played for both the Cubs and the Mets. As a result, I got a free dinner for eight at the Normandy Inn!

I decided to have the dinner on a Monday night, and I invited Louie Dampier and his first wife, Marty; Artis and Enola Gilmore; and fellow teammate Walt Simon and his wife, Marge, to join us. Cheri had gone to the doctor that morning. It was close to her due date, but the doctor said, "No, you're not quite there yet. Make an appointment to see me next Monday." She did, and we went out that night for dinner.

Around five o'clock the next morning, Cheri woke me up and said, "I don't feel right. I don't know if the baby's coming or not." I told her, "You're not used to all that rich food. You're probably just having indigestion. Go back to sleep." I'm not sure if she went back to sleep, but I did. About two hours later, she woke up again and insisted, "We'd better go." So, we went to the hospital, and sure enough our daughter, Sheridan, was born around noon that day.

Back then, husbands weren't allowed in the delivery room, so I was sitting in the waiting room with Cheri's mother, whom we had called. One of the nurses came out to let us know that the baby had been born and invited us to the newborn nursery to have our first look. I had already figured out that if the baby was wrapped in a pink blanket, it was a girl, and

Cheri and me with baby Sheridan at our home in Louisville.

if it was in a blue blanket, it was a boy. When one of the nursery workers held her up, she was wrapped in a pink blanket and looked exactly like my father.

The Colonels had a game the day of Sheridan's birth, so I left the hospital to head to Freedom Hall. After the game, I was usually the last guy out of the locker room because I'd sit and cool off before taking a shower. But that night I was the first guy out because I wanted to get back to the hospital to see Cheri and Sheridan. There was always a large group of people outside Freedom Hall who would gather for autographs and pictures. I usually stopped to sign autographs and pose for photographs, but that night I was in such a hurry to get to the hospital that I rushed past everyone. The next day, a woman wrote a letter to the editor of the *Courier-Journal,* asking, "Who did Dan Issel think he was? What a big shot, not having time to sign autographs for the kids?" It was a lesson I learned early on: if you don't take the time to appreciate the fans, it'll come back to bite you.

Having a baby girl was a huge change in our lives. We'd put her in the car seat and take her to dinner, and by about three weeks old she was sleeping through the night. She was such a good girl, a real blessing to Cheri and me. Florence Armstrong, Cheri's aunt, came up with the idea of naming her Sheridan. It was a clever blend of Cheri and Dan, so we thought it was pretty cool—combining our first names together. For her middle name, Lynn, we were inspired by Cheri's sister, Vicki, who also has Lynn as her middle name.

Another highlight in the first month of 1972 was the ABA All-Star Game, which was held in Freedom Hall on January 29. The game was set to be nationally televised, and at the shootaround that day, our general manager, Mike Storen, told me I had to wear Adidas, the league's official shoe. I explained to Mike that I couldn't do that because I was under contract with Keds to wear their blue suede PRO-Keds sneakers. He then asked if I could at least wear white shoes, and I agreed. The only white PRO-Keds they could find were a size 14, but since I wore a size 15, I ended up playing in shoes that were a size too small.

As for the game itself, the East team featured Artis, Louie, Julius Erving, Rick Barry, and me—basically a Who's Who of the Naismith Hall of Fame. The East won the game 142–115, but there was some controversy over who should have been named MVP. Jim McDaniels, a rookie with the Carolina Cougars, scored twenty-four points for the East, while I added a second-best twenty-one. I had scored most of my points early, when the game was still close, while Jim, coming off the bench, scored eighteen in the fourth quarter, after the game had already been decided. A lot of people thought I'd win the MVP because there were more Louisville fans voting, but I later found out that members of the media voted me in by a narrow margin: 20–19.[2] My MVP award was a huge sword mounted on a board, a full-size refrigerator, and a color television.

The impact of Artis joining the Colonels was significant. During my rookie year, I had been playing center, but when Artis signed in my second year, I moved to the forward position, and that really freed me up defensively. Artis was terrific. Julius Erving and George McGinnis both entered the ABA the same year, but who was the Rookie of the Year? Artis. He was also the MVP of the league in his rookie year.

Playing against Artis in practice every day taught me two major lessons. First, on the defensive end, I learned that you can't let a good big man get the position they want on the low post. So, I made it a point to beat Artis down the floor. That habit paid off later when I faced guys like Kareem Abdul-Jabbar and other great centers in the NBA. I'd get to the spot before they could, forcing them to set up a foot or two farther out than they were comfortable. That small adjustment made a big difference in defending them effectively.

Second, on the offensive end, I realized there was no way I could consistently battle those same dominant centers in the low post with my back to the basket. If I tried, I'd just end up getting my shot sent right back at me, so I developed an intermediate-range game. I found it was to my advantage to draw bigger centers out onto the floor, into areas where they weren't as comfortable defensively. All of that started with those daily matchups against Artis in practice.

While those practices with Artis helped shape the finer points of my game, actual ABA games were a different story. Fights weren't uncommon, and two of our toughest opponents were John Brisker and Warren Jabali.

One of my favorite John Brisker stories happened when he was playing for the Pittsburgh Condors. He got into a fight during practice, stormed off to the locker room, and someone said, "Hey, Brisker's got a gun in his locker!" Sure enough, he came back out onto the practice floor with a pistol in hand. But by then, everyone else had taken off running. They knew better than to stick around when Brisker was coming back angry and armed!

Brisker would literally try to hurt people in games. Tom Nissalke was coaching the Dallas Chaparrals at the time, and before one game against Brisker he said, "I'll give $500 to anyone who knocks him out." Len Chappell, one of the Dallas players, asked to be put in the starting lineup. Everyone figured he'd take a hard foul or something. But when they lined up for the opening tip, as soon as the ref tossed the ball, Chappell just coldcocked Brisker—knocked him out right there at center court! The game started with Brisker laid out in the jump circle. After the game, Chappell collected $500 from Nissalke.

Another tough guy was Warren Jabali, who was known as Warren Armstrong when he played at Wichita State. Incredibly talented, he played for just about every team in the ABA, including attending the Colonels' training camp during my rookie year. Teams put up with him only because of how good he was. But even with all that talent, he didn't make it out of training camp in Kentucky. They let him go before the season even started.

One night, Louie Dampier and I were playing for the Colonels in Denver. We ended up at the same restaurant as Jabali. He had a big group with him, maybe eight or ten people. Louie and I were off to the side at a table for two. At the end of the meal, Jabali stood up and said to the waiter, "I didn't leave you a tip because we're all struggling on different levels." The waiter thought he was joking. He checked the bill and started picking up plates, looking for a tip. Sure enough, Jabali hadn't left a dime. That was his way of saying, "You're not getting a tip." Just flat-out mean.

When my third season with the Colonels rolled around, we had a bad taste in our mouths from the way the previous season ended. Joe Mullaney was still our coach, and the roster remained largely the same. Expectations were high because we believed we had the best team in the ABA and were poised for a championship.

The All-Star Game in my third year took place at the Salt Palace in Salt Lake City on February 6, 1973. The night before, comedian Bill Cosby performed at the arena as part of the All-Star festivities. Heavy fog delayed his arrival into the city,[3] so Cosby showed up around an hour late. When he finally took the stage, he was dressed in blue jeans and a baggy white sweater, but he had the crowd laughing in no time. As for the game itself, Artis, Louie, and I represented the Colonels as selections to the East roster. However, the West team got the best of us, led by twenty-six points from Willie Wise of the Utah Stars.

Around that time, there was a lot of movement between the ABA and the NBA. Charlie Scott made the jump to the NBA after his rookie year. At the start of my third season, Julius Erving signed a contract with the Atlanta Hawks, but a judge voided it because the Hawks didn't hold his draft rights. I spoke with my attorney, J. Bruce Miller, who reached out to Jerry Colangelo of the Phoenix Suns about the possibility of me moving to the NBA. The deal was practically set, but I couldn't go through with it. Cheri and I had talked it over, and we didn't want to leave Kentucky, especially with our young daughter. Cheri's family was in Lexington, and in the end we decided it was best to stay. Years later, Jerry Colangelo told me he still had that contract in his desk.

We finished the 1972–73 season with a record of 56–28, which was one game behind our Eastern Division rivals, the Carolina Cougars. The Cougars had a strong team, including Joe Caldwell, Billy Cunningham, and Matt Calvin, an All-Star guard in the ABA. It was also Larry Brown's first year as their coach.

Our first-round opponent was the Virginia Squires, who not only had Julius Erving but had also acquired George Gervin during the season. However, we handled them fairly easily, winning the series four games to one. In the Eastern Division finals, we faced off against the Carolina Cougars. In game six of that series, my teammate Wendell Ladner, a small forward, intercepted a pass and tossed it to point guard Jim O'Brien. As Wendell sailed out of bounds, he crashed into a five-gallon glass water cooler behind the bench and got badly cut up. There was blood everywhere. He needed forty-two stitches in the locker room, most of them to his left arm and lower back.[4] Despite the injury, once he was stitched up, he wanted to get back in and play! We won that game 119–100. Three days later, we closed out the series by besting the Cougars on their home court, 107–96. Artis picked up his third and fourth fouls early in the third quarter,[5] but the rest of us stepped up. I scored thirty-one points, Rick Mount added seventeen, and Walt Simon chipped in fifteen.

Our victory secured us another chance to win the ABA title against our arch nemesis, the Pacers. That series also went to seven games, but the Pacers came out on top in the decisive game seven, winning 88–81 in Freedom Hall. It wasn't our best showing, as reflected in the fact that we scored just eleven points in the third quarter. Artis led our team with nineteen points and seventeen rebounds. George McGinnis of the Pacers finished with twenty-seven points and was named MVP of the ABA playoffs. After the game, veteran Pacers small forward Roger Brown called out the Colonels. "I think they got the jitters," he told a sports reporter. "They shouldn't have—they've been in a seventh game before, haven't they?"[6]

Yes, we had. But things were about to change.

6

Finally, a Championship

I missed watching Secretariat's dominant performance in person at the 1973 Kentucky Derby because we were on a bus back from our championship series against the Pacers. However, Cheri and I had made plane and hotel reservations to watch him run in the Belmont Stakes in New York.

Just a few days before the Belmont, Cheri's sister, Vicki, was in a serious car accident in Lexington. She was driving her Ford Pinto, which had a sunroof, and was attempting to cross a four-lane highway. A nearby car was turning, so she proceeded across, not realizing there was a plumbing truck coming in the other lane. The truck struck her car.

Vicki was thrown through the sunroof, and the plumbing truck came to rest on her chest. Thankfully, it landed in the grassy median. Had it landed on the pavement, she likely wouldn't have survived. Some Good Samaritans rushed over and managed to lift the truck and pull her out from under the wheel.

As soon as we got word of the accident, we rushed to the hospital from our home in Louisville. The doctors didn't give Vicki much of a chance, but her strong physical condition worked in her favor. Vicki had undergone a tracheotomy, so she couldn't speak, and the ICU staff only allowed us to visit her for about fifteen minutes at a time, three times a day. During those brief visits Vicki kept walking her fingers across her chest. We had no idea what she was trying to tell us.

When I was a Colonel, the first horses I owned were harness horses at the Red Mile in Lexington. I really enjoyed jogging them on my own.

About a week later, once she had recovered enough to speak again, we asked her about it. She told us she had been trying to say, "I'm okay. Go on and go to the Belmont." That's what the finger-walking gesture meant! But of course, we didn't go. We watched the Belmont on television instead, and just as we had while watching Secretariat's Preakness on television, we witnessed another historic performance.

After the 1972–73 season, Cheri and I were naive enough to believe we'd be in Louisville for the rest of our lives, so we decided to build our dream home. Cheri has always had a keen eye for design, so while we both discussed the features we wanted in our home, she took charge. We began by finding a lot not far from our home in Green Springs—just a couple of miles up the road, on Wolf Pen Trace in eastern Jefferson County. It was a dead-end street with about thirteen available lots. We bought one of them, and Cheri collaborated with an architect to draw up the plans.

We then found a builder, Bob McDonald, who was a huge Colonels fan, and he ended up constructing the house. We designed the house specifically for our needs. It featured eight-foot doorways, ten-foot ceilings, a raised vanity so I didn't have to bend so far over to brush my teeth, and a seven-foot showerhead in the bathroom. The exterior was white brick with white columns, and Cheri handpicked every detail—from the light fixtures to the knobs on the kitchen cabinets. She devoted a lot of time to the design, and the entire project took thirteen months to complete.

During the early stages of our home construction, rumors started circulating that the Colonels were up for sale. Apparently, a reporter from the *Courier-Journal* posed a question to team co-owner David Jones that no one had ever asked before: "What does the average attendance have to be at a Colonels game to break even?" Jones then called co-owner Wendell Cherry to ask him the same thing. After the reporter left, Wendell came in and told David, "We could sell out Freedom Hall every game and still lose money." David's response was simple: "Sell the team."

Jones and Cherry reached an agreement with a group of potential owners who planned to move the Colonels to Cincinnati once Riverfront Coliseum was completed. In the meantime, as part of the arrangement, we would play ten of our forty-two home games at the University of Cincinnati's Armory Fieldhouse. The story goes that one morning John Y. Brown III, the son of John Y. Brown Jr., came to the breakfast table in tears, upset that his favorite team—the Colonels—was going to leave Louisville. In response, his parents, John Y. and Ellie Brown, decided to buy the team back. Their decision wasn't about making a profit, but rather about demonstrating their commitment to Louisville. They assumed ownership in the summer of 1973. Nobody on our team wanted to play ten home games in Cincinnati, and I certainly didn't want to stick around if they were moving there. At the time, though, many people believed that the Browns taking over the Colonels was a great move—it would keep the team in Louisville and provide financial stability. John had sold his stake in Kentucky Fried Chicken a couple of years earlier for hundreds of millions of dollars, so it seemed like a solid plan.

The organization's culture definitely shifted. It became evident that John had handed the team over to Ellie. She appointed an almost entirely female-led board of directors, consisting of prominent women from Louisville, with the only male member being Coach Rupp. The board's main responsibility was to sell season tickets, but it was clear that John would still have the final say. Mike Storen left to become the commissioner of the ABA, and ironically, they hired Gene Rhodes as the new general manager. Gene was the coach Storen had fired just a couple of years earlier. Joe Mullaney also departed, though it's unclear whether he left voluntarily or was let go. I do recall one of his quotes, though: "I don't want to work for a man who knows more about frying chicken than he does about professional basketball." That's when they brought in Babe McCarthy as the new coach for my fourth season with the Colonels.

McCarthy was a players' coach. He was laid-back and had a noticeable Southern drawl. My teammates and I weren't thrilled with Mullaney as coach, especially after our second season. Many players felt our game plan was lacking. For example, when we played the Nets, whenever Artis, Louie, or I had the ball, a second defender would often come over to guard us. They basically said, "Anyone else can step up and beat us, but we're not going to let Artis, Louie, or Dan beat us." Meanwhile, on the other end of the court, the Nets had two players who could win the series almost singlehandedly: Rick Barry and John Roche. Our defensive strategy was to guard those two one-on-one, while our best players were getting double-teamed on offense. I'm not sure if anyone directly said anything, but I think Mullaney lost the locker room after that series, even though we bounced back and made it to the finals the following year. Everyone seemed to be happy that Babe was the new coach heading into the 1973–74 season.

In the postseason, we swept the Carolina Cougars in the Eastern Division semifinals. However, game two of the series had to be postponed because an F4-strength tornado tore through Louisville on the afternoon of April 3. I was taking my pregame nap—a routine I always followed on game days—when the tornado siren went off. Sheridan was just a toddler, so Cheri and I scooped her up and the three of us headed for the basement. We could already hear it coming.

ABA champs! The official team photograph of the 1975 Kentucky Colonels.

I'd heard tornadoes described as sounding like a freight train barreling toward you. Well, that's exactly what it sounded like. We watched through a small basement window as the twister passed just six blocks behind our house. It looked more like a dark cloud moving along the ground, swirling with debris. And then, after it passed, there was this strange, eerie silence. The only sounds were the cries of injured farm animals, mostly cows mooing in distress.

When we turned on the radio, we learned that the storm had ripped part of the roof off of Freedom Hall. It had killed two people, injured over two hundred others, and caused millions of dollars in damage to homes and businesses.[1]

Maybe that event was an omen for our team, because in the next round the New York Nets swept us in the Eastern Division finals. By that time, the Nets had Julius Erving, and they had the best record in the ABA that year. I remember we were in New York, sitting in Babe's room playing cards. We were down in the series, and John Y. Brown and David Vance came in and saw us playing cards. It really rubbed John Y. the wrong way. He thought we should've been watching game films or practicing instead. That moment pretty much marked the end of the Babe McCarthy era—it lasted just one year. Not long after he left the Colonels, Babe was diagnosed with prostate cancer and passed away at age fifty-one. I enjoyed playing for him.

The following season was historic. To me, the only difference between the years of futility—losing in the championship round a couple of times, getting upset in the early rounds in other years—and winning the championship in 1975 was Hubie Brown. His attention to detail was incredible. He had us analyze past games and break down plays. I played for four Hall of Fame coaches during my career, but Hubie was the best at preparation. Stan Albeck, our assistant coach, was responsible for charting all of our plays. He'd sit on the bench with a yellow pad, tracking everything—how he did it, I don't know. But when we walked into the locker room before a game, the plays we had run against that opponent the last time, how many times we ran them, and how successful they were would be written on the board. Hubie also gave us a playbook—the first time any Colonels coach had done that. It included rules about being on time, how to dress on the road, and fines for breaking those rules. It was the most organized the team had ever been.

Hiring Hubie that year was definitely the turning point for us. Hubie was all business—there was no messing around with him. When it was time to work, nothing else mattered. He also had a rule: if a player walked into a restaurant or bar after a game and saw Hubie there, he had to turn around and leave. The same applied if Hubie walked in and saw a player—he would turn around and leave. That way, at least in his mind, he was protecting both his own privacy and that of the players.

His directness could sometimes rub people the wrong way. In 1975, you never used the F-word in public. One time, we had a practice that was open to any woman who was interested in the Colonels and wanted to watch. Ellie Brown was there, along with the board and other influential women from the community. As the practice started, the ladies were chatting among themselves. It felt more like a social event than a practice because of the background noise. Hubie blew his whistle and said, "We're having this practice for you. If you're interested in what we're doing here, then I'd appreciate it if you'd pay attention. But if you insist on talking, I'd like for you to get the f—— out of here." I guarantee you, for the rest of the practice those ladies didn't say a word!

We improved as the 1974–75 campaign progressed, winning our last nine regular-season games and defeating the Nets in a one-game playoff to secure the number one seed in the Eastern Division. In one of those final regular-season games, we played the Nets at Freedom Hall. One of their small forwards, Wendell Ladner, and I got into a shoving match, and I

Discussing game strategy with Coach Hubie Brown during a timeout. (Photograph by Mark Gordon.)

landed a pretty solid right-hand punch. He hit me under the chin in return, and I ended up needing Steri-Strips. After the game, I got five stitches in my chin. The funny part of the story, though, is that my teammate Ron Thomas was kind of our enforcer. Ladner and I had been throwing punches not far from our bench, so after the game, as I was getting my chin stitched up, I asked, "Ron, where were you? Why didn't you come out to help me?"

He replied, "Dan, didn't you hear? The league said if anyone leaves the bench to fight, they get fined $25."

I said, "Ron, the next time I get in a fight, you get your tail out there, and I'll give you $100." Incidentally, it was rare for an ABA game to go by without a fight. That's just how it was.

In the Eastern Division finals, we beat the Spirits of St. Louis in five games to secure our spot in the ABA Finals, where we once again faced the Pacers. Eleven days before the Finals began, John Y. and Ellie Brown hosted a Kentucky Derby party at their Louisville home. Former sports broadcaster Howard Cosell was there to film a ten- to fifteen-minute live segment for ABC, capturing the atmosphere of a traditional Derby party in Louisville. The event was packed with celebrities, big names at

I landed a solid punch on Wendell Ladner, but I was the one who ended up with stitches in my chin. (Photograph by Mark Gordon.)

Before our title win, a few teammates and I joined Muhammad Ali and Howard Cosell at a Kentucky Derby party hosted by John Y. Brown. (© Bill Luster, USA Today Network via Imagn Images.)

the time. However, they didn't invite the entire Colonels team—just our general manager, David Vance, Coach Hubie Brown, Louie Dampier, Artis Gilmore, and me.

Muhammad Ali, a Louisville native, showed up with his entourage. Between the kitchen and the dining room, there was a narrow pantry, maybe four or five feet wide and about twenty feet long. When they arrived, they went straight into that pantry and stayed there, quietly talking among themselves. Then the camera lights came on. Howard Cosell was about to do his big segment when, suddenly, out comes Ali from the pantry—loud and animated. He had a fight coming up in Vegas against Ron Lyle, and in classic Ali fashion he starts shouting, "Howard! I'm gonna kill him! He's got no chance!"

He completely hijacked Howard's segment, took over the whole thing on national television. Eventually, Howard got a few words in with John Y. and that was it. The lights went off, and just like that Ali returned to the

Putting up an easy basket against George McGinnis (30) and Len Elmore in the championship game. (Photograph by Mark Gordon.)

pantry and stayed there for the rest of the night, almost like an introvert. It was hilarious in the moment. I had the chance to be around Ali a few times, and I truly believe he was naturally shy. But when the cameras were on, he came alive. Watching that transformation was fascinating.

Game one against the Pacers tipped off on May 13. We came out strong, winning the first three games of the series. In game three, as it was nearing the end, I was lined up next to George McGinnis while one of my teammates was shooting a free throw. George glanced at me and said, "Looks like it's finally going to be your turn," since we were about to take a 3–0 lead in the series.

Prior to game four we were in the locker room when our general manager, David Vance, walked in. Artis and I were sitting next to each other, and David said, "Wouldn't it be great if we won this championship back home in front of our fans?" Now, I'm not saying that Artis intentionally threw the game, but we didn't get his best effort in game four after David's comment. We lost that game, then came back to Freedom Hall and won game five to clinch the championship, 110–105, in front of over sixteen thousand fans.

In any sport, when one team wins the first three games, loses the fourth, and then wins the series in the fifth game, I like to call it the "Artis Gilmore Sweep." I truly believe that if we had gotten Artis's full effort, we would have wrapped it up in four games in Indianapolis. Instead, we had to go back home for game five, which we won behind a thirty-one-point performance from Artis.

I'll never forget how family members, friends, and fans flooded the court after the final buzzer sounded. I remember hugging Cheri, and we stood there for a while soaking in the atmosphere before finally heading back to the locker room. Louie and I were the only former UK players on that championship team, but we took pride in helping bring a title to the City of Louisville and the state of Kentucky, especially after coming so close in previous years with such good teams. It was a huge moment. In his *Courier-Journal* story about our victory, sports reporter Dave Kindred asked Louie how it felt to be a champion—his first at any level of basketball. "I'm stunned right now," he said.[2] "Ask me in about an hour."

Even Hubie chimed in. During a speech he gave while standing at center court with the Browns and Kentucky governor Julian Carroll, he said, "I would like to thank 13 dedicated people—the 10 players, two

Chaos erupts at Freedom Hall after the Colonels win the championship, with team owner Ellie Brown and Kentucky governor Julian Carroll leading the way. (Photograph by Mark Gordon.)

coaches and the trainer. A lot of unselfishness, dedication and a helluva lot of camaraderie went into this championship."[3]

After everyone had showered and left Freedom Hall, we all headed to Larry Jones's house for a party. Larry and his twin brother, Harry, had both played football at UK and were big Kentucky Colonels boosters. The party went on and on. In fact, when Cheri and I finally left, the sun was just coming up. We had a babysitter named Ann Holcomb, and this is how spoiled we were—she was like part of the family. She'd come over early enough so that she'd be there when Sheridan woke up, letting Cheri and me sleep in. Ann always joked, "When you win the championship, I'm going to come up and throw a pan of water on you to get you up early." Sure enough, Cheri and I had only been asleep for about three hours when Ann walked into our bedroom with a pan of water and splashed it on me to wake me up, fully knowing she'd have to clean up the mess. That was definitely a rude awakening the morning after our championship game! But Ann kept her word.

While we were celebrating our hard-earned championship, there were some difficult realities within the team that couldn't be ignored. One of those was Jim Bradley. A former standout forward at Northern Illinois University, he possessed immense talent, on par with the likes of Julius Erving and David Thompson. However, he struggled with drug addiction. He was consistently late to everything, and Hubie kept fining him. By the end of the season the fine pool was about $7,000—most of it from Jim. We used that money to fund a postseason team meal at the Normandy Inn to celebrate our title. Despite his issues, Jim was incredibly gifted. Had he gotten his life together, he could have been one of the best. Unfortunately, after his career he was shot and killed in a drug deal gone wrong.

That summer, I started hearing rumors about John Y. Brown possibly breaking up the Colonels roster. Supposedly, the only two assets he had that he could sell to make up for potential losses were me or Artis, and the decision seemed to be going back and forth. Someone allegedly suggested that he should sell me because he thought Artis's career would last much longer than mine.

To understand why the Colonels were even considering breaking up a championship roster, it's important to look at the financial pressures facing the team and the league at the time. One of the early problems the ABA faced was that teams would give away tickets or charge low prices just to fill the stands. The idea was to create the appearance of a crowd and generate interest. The Kentucky Colonels, in particular, ran into issues with this. I've had several people tell me that when they were kids they could get into a Colonels game for just fifty cents. The problem was that fans got used to attending games for next to nothing.

As the quality of the league improved and player salaries increased—especially after the team brought in players like me and Artis Gilmore—ticket prices had to go up. But the fans never fully adjusted to the idea of paying more. As players, we could get as many complimentary tickets as we needed, within reason. For some reason, the team used a hole punch to mark the complimentary tickets.

I had a good friend, Bill Fox, who worked with me at Citizens Fidelity Bank. He used to call and ask, "You got any of those tickets with the holes in them?" That was his way of saying he wanted to come to the game but didn't want to pay for it.

This mindset became a problem. So, even when we won the championship in the 1974–75 season, the franchise still lost money. The combination of low ticket revenue and the lack of a national television contract really hurt the bottom line for all ABA teams, and it directly affected my career path.

One day in September, Cheri, Sheridan, and I were at the former harness track Louisville Downs, which is now a training center for Churchill Downs. Ironically, Stuart Jay, one of the investors who purchased the Colonels from the original owners, came up to our table and said, "You, Louie, and Artis should buy the franchise from John Y. and then fold the team and sell yourselves to the NBA. You'd make some money doing that." We all laughed about it, and then he left the table. Soon after that, I was paged to the press box at the racetrack, and I knew that wouldn't be good news. I picked up the phone in the press room at Louisville Downs, and it was Ellie Brown on the line. I'll never forget what she said. She said, "Dan, this is the hardest thing I've ever had to do, but we've traded you to the Baltimore Claws." I replied, "Ellie, are you aware that I have a no-trade clause in my contract?" She cupped her hand over the phone and said, "John, you better get on the phone." So, John got on and basically said the same thing. I told him, "I have a no-trade clause in my contract; I don't think you can do this," and I hung up. Incidentally, although my trade clause was enforceable, I chose not to enforce it.

We left the racetrack and went to the home of my attorney, J. Bruce Miller. It was a Friday evening, and Bruce was sitting at the kitchen table in shorts and a T-shirt. I told him what had happened, and by then there was a scrolling banner at the bottom of the television screen announcing that I'd been traded, with the full story coming on the eleven o'clock news. Bruce said, "Well, I don't have any beer, so let's walk down to the 7-Eleven." As we were heading out, Bruce added, "You don't want to go home because there'll be news cameras. Stay the night here with us." Just as we were leaving, Cheri called out that Sheridan still needed a pacifier to fall asleep, so we walked to 7-Eleven. I was wearing a coat and tie, and Bruce was in shorts and a T-shirt. We bought some pipe tobacco for Bruce, a six-pack of beer, and two pacifiers. The guy at the counter looked at us and said, "Man, I don't know what kind of party you're having, but I wish I was invited." We laughed and replied, "No, this is no party." After that, we went back to Bruce's and spent the night.

The Baltimore Claws was the former Memphis Sounds ABA franchise, purchased by a group of businesspeople in Baltimore and set to debut in the 1975–76 season. This transaction highlighted the ABA's ongoing financial struggles. For example, even though the Colonels won the 1975 ABA championship, they still weren't making any money, so you can imagine what kind of financial situation the rest of the league was in. The Claws owners convinced us to fly up and meet with them, and they held a press conference at Pimlico Race Course. Given my love for horses, they thought the venue would impress me. Bruce was able to negotiate some terms on our behalf, but it was an uncomfortable situation to say the least. I never imagined I'd have to play anywhere other than Kentucky. I remember reading the word "commensurate" in my contract. The owners said they would find us housing in Baltimore that was "commensurate" with what we had in Louisville. It would've been hard to find, because our home in Louisville was gorgeous and custom-built just for us. Ironically, Joe Mullaney, who had been my coach for two years with the Colonels, was now the coach of the Baltimore Claws. They had some older players I knew well, like Mel Daniels and George Carter. They had some decent players, but everyone knew this was a no-go. In training camp as a Colonel, we usually had two practice sessions a day. But in Baltimore we only had one practice in the morning. Mel, George, and Joe would head to the former Bowie Race Track for the afternoon.

In the meantime, the situation was taking a toll on me and my family. We were staying in a hotel room in downtown Baltimore—me, Cheri, Sheridan, our family dog, and a parakeet. Every afternoon, I'd return to the room and Cheri would be in tears over the potential homes she'd been shown for us to live in. During this time, it was difficult to see God's plan for our lives. However, as we discovered, it couldn't have turned out better. After about ten days, I got a call from John Y. He said, "Dan, if I get you out of Baltimore, will you say something nice about me in the media back in Louisville?" He and Ellie were getting hammered in the media for this decision. I told him, "John, get me out of here and I'll say anything you want me to say." He replied, "Good. I'm here at the hotel, come down to room 212." I later found out that he had never been paid the money promised by the Claws franchise. The deal he had negotiated fell through. The Nuggets, with their outstanding team, had a rookie center, Marvin Webster, who fell sick with a form of hepatitis, so they were looking for a replacement center. John Y. worked out a deal for the Nuggets to acquire me. After ten days in Baltimore, we were on a plane to Denver. We had been in the process of moving our furniture to Baltimore, and the moving company had already left Louisville. When we called, we told them to turn the truck around and head to Denver instead. Meanwhile, Baltimore played just three exhibition games before the whole franchise folded. I definitely dodged a bullet.

My family and I were disappointed about leaving Kentucky, but we understood how bad the situation in Baltimore was, so we were relieved to get out of there. Moving to Denver was a real blessing, as it was one of the more solid franchises in the ABA. In 1974, Carl Scheer, who had previously been with the Carolina Cougars in the ABA, came to Denver and formed a limited partnership to buy what was then the Denver Rockets. Aware that there was already an NBA team called the Rockets, he quickly changed the name to the Nuggets. He also brought in Larry Brown as head coach and Doug Moe as assistant coach. I knew Doug and Larry from playing against them. I knew they were excellent coaches, but what really impressed me was the sheer talent we had on that Nuggets team. The biggest coup Scheer pulled off was signing David Thompson, who had been the number one NBA draft pick by the Atlanta Hawks in 1975. I was excited to be joining a situation like that, but it still wasn't Kentucky. In the end, though, it turned out to be the best thing that could have happened to us.

As a family, we adjusted to Denver pretty quickly. We enrolled Sheridan in preschool, and because of that we made friends outside of the Nuggets organization—some of whom remain close friends to this day. We bought a townhouse. While it wasn't as spacious as the house we left behind in Louisville, it was in a great area and had security. One thing we had expected was to be knee-deep in snow for most of the winter. While the nearby mountains do get that kind of snow, we quickly learned that the climate in Denver is actually milder than Kentucky's during the winter months.

One of the things we negotiated before moving to Baltimore was adding a few perks to the contract. One of the most valuable was that Sheridan's schooling would be covered. So, for the entire time she was in preschool and later elementary school, the Nuggets paid for her private education. That was about the only positive outcome from our ten days in Baltimore.

November 2, 1975, was my first trip back to Freedom Hall after being traded to the Nuggets. We were playing the Colonels, and John Tong, who was the public address announcer for both the Colonels and the University of Louisville for years, was on the mic. He introduced our two guards first, then they introduced me, and I received an incredible ovation from the Colonels fans. The applause was so overwhelming it sent chills up and down my spine. I'll never forget John Tong announcing, "And at forward, Bobby Jones."

Larry Brown, who was holding Bobby Jones on the bench, refused to let him come out while the crowd's applause for me continued. John Tong repeated, "And at forward, Bobby Jones" about five times before the ovation finally started to subside. Only then did Larry allow Bobby to run onto the court!

Later that season we faced the Colonels in the 1976 ABA semifinals and managed to beat them. As a result, I ended up being part of the final game the Kentucky Colonels ever played—only, I was wearing a Nuggets uniform. That summer, four ABA teams joined the NBA: the Nuggets, the Spurs, the Pacers, and the Nets. The remaining ABA teams folded, including the Colonels and the Spirits of St. Louis.

There's an old story that John Y. Brown tried to find twenty people to put up $50,000 each for part ownership of the Colonels. Apparently, a few people offered to buy multiple shares, saying, "Okay, I'll take five shares," but Brown insisted on having twenty individual investors. When he couldn't find them, he decided to fold the franchise. I was certainly sorry to see that. The only championship I ever won was with them.

The Spirits of St. Louis, meanwhile, was owned by two brothers, Ozzie and Daniel Silna, who made their fortune in the polyester industry. The brothers agreed to dissolve the Spirits of St. Louis in exchange for $2.2 million up front and, more importantly, one-seventh of the national television revenue from the four ABA teams that joined the NBA.[4] At the time, that wasn't much money. NBA games were often aired on tape delay, sometimes after the evening news. But the key part of the deal was that their cut was in perpetuity. Forever.

As the NBA grew—especially with the explosion of television deals in the 1980s, 1990s, and 2000s—that "small cut" became massive. The Silnas had no team, no front office, no players, no overhead. Just a mailbox where the checks came. In 2014, the NBA reached a final settlement with the brothers to the tune of $500 million. By that time, it was estimated that they had earned around $800 million without ever owning an NBA franchise.[5] It was arguably the greatest sports business deal ever made.

Our Nuggets team found success in the NBA right from the start. In fact, we won the Midwest Division in our first two years in the league. However, I did notice a shift in culture as we transitioned from the ABA to the NBA. In the ABA, we were the underdogs, constantly fighting for recognition, and that struggle created a unique bond and camaraderie. But that sense of unity felt different in the NBA. I'm not sure if it was because there were more teams, or if it was simply because NBA teams were generally more financially stable and didn't have to worry about their franchises folding.

Not only did the ABA produce great players and legendary coaches, but it also gave rise to some outstanding announcers. Take Marty Brennaman, for example. Before becoming the longtime radio voice of the Cincinnati Reds, he was the announcer for the Virginia Squires during the era of Charlie Scott, George Gervin, and Julius Erving. And then there's Bob Costas. He was just twenty-two years old when he became the play-by-play announcer for the Spirits of St. Louis. Of course, Bob went on to become one of the iconic sports broadcasters of our time. Even today, he remains an ABA guy through and through. Bob serves on the board of the Dropping Dimes Foundation, which was cofounded by Scott Tarter in Indianapolis. The foundation provides support to former ABA players who have fallen on hard times.

In our first year in the NBA, fans voted to determine the starting lineup for the 1977 All-Star Game in Milwaukee. Since the Nuggets were brand new to the league, our management team decided to stuff the ballot box. The Nuggets' office staff would host All-Star voting parties, bringing in pizza and soda, and everyone who worked for the team would spend a couple of hours filling out ballots. As a result, the Nuggets had three starters in the 1977 All-Star game: me, David Thompson, and Bobby Jones, along with Paul Westphal and Norm Van Lier. Half of both rosters were former ABA players. However, the game itself was the most miserable basketball experience I've ever had. The game before the All-Star game, we played in Los Angeles, and I scored over thirty points against Kareem Abdul-Jabbar. I was having a solid enough season to make the All-Star team, but I wasn't good enough to start in front of Kareem. To make matters worse—and this is important to note—Kareem had played in Milwaukee before joining the Lakers. He said he'd forgotten his warmups, so he came out in a Milwaukee Bucks warmup suit, even though he was playing for the Lakers. When they announced me as a starter, I got booed unmercifully. My only NBA All-Star game was certainly not an enjoyable experience. I played ten minutes without scoring a point, while Kareem scored twenty-one.

As our team settled into the NBA, my personal life underwent a shift as well, with news that brought us even closer together as a family. Cheri and I had been trying for quite some time to have another child, but we weren't sure if it would happen. One day in March of 1978 Cheri had a doctor's appointment because she thought she might be pregnant. I was at practice, and after it ended I called her from the office of our trainer, Robert "Chopper" Travaglini. That's when I received the exciting news—she was pregnant! We were overjoyed at the thought of having a second child. Later that day, we called my parents and Cheri's parents. We let Sheridan get on the phone to tell them that she was going to be a big sister.

Back then they didn't do ultrasounds, so we didn't know the baby's gender in advance. When Sheridan was born, I had to wait in the waiting room, but by the time our second child was on the way, I could go in with Cheri while she was in labor. The medical staff was using a fetal heart monitor to check the baby's heartbeat, which ranged between 166 and 172 beats per minute. Our pediatrician, Dr. Stanley Goodman, told us, "If the heart rate is under 160, it's usually a boy, and if it's over 160, it's usually a girl." So, I was convinced we were having another girl. In the delivery room, I held Cheri's hand and focused on her face. As the baby emerged, Dr. Goodman exclaimed, "The plumbing's on the outside!" The date was October 9, 1978, and we named our son Scott Cody Issel—Scott after my brother Greg's middle name and Cody in honor of my college friend, Steve Cody. His birth was a long-awaited moment for us, especially with nearly a seven-year gap between him and Sheridan. Life couldn't have been better.

I don't recall basing our parenting style on anyone specific. Both Cheri and I grew up in loving, supportive families, so I think we had a pretty good sense of the kind of parents we wanted to be. I give Cheri all the credit, though, because I was traveling so much. When I was on the road, I'd call home every morning to check in—to make sure everything was okay, that everyone had made it through the night and gotten off to school. If we were playing on the East Coast, I'd usually call again after the game, since they'd often watched it, and we'd do a little recap of how

I played. If we were out West, it was usually too late to call Cheri and the kids, so I'd wait until the next morning.

But once I got into coaching and cell phones became more common, communication got a lot easier. Cheri could call me anytime, or I could reach out to her during the day if something came up. Being a professional athlete and traveling so much, I missed a lot of things the kids were involved in: school plays, sporting events, milestones like that. Cheri was incredible; she kept everything running smoothly at home while I was away. But the best part was that from early summer through early fall, I was home all day, every day. So, in a way, it balanced out. When the kids were out of school, I could be there for everything—every game, every event, all the day-to-day stuff.

7

My Journey in the Mile High City

Denver is a great sports town. Today, the city supports all of its professional franchises, but it wasn't always that way. The Denver Broncos have always been, and likely always will be, the city's favorite team because they were Denver's first real connection to professional sports.

Season tickets to Broncos games have been sold out for decades. When I first arrived in Denver, the Nuggets were just becoming the city's second professional franchise. At the time, the NBA didn't have nearly the popularity it enjoys today.

Early on, there wasn't a whole lot of interest in the Nuggets, at least not until the Broncos' season ended. But as the Denver population grew, so did the sports landscape. Today, the city is home to a lot of transplants, people who moved here from other parts of the country and brought their own team loyalties with them. When the Lakers come to town, for example, you'll see almost as many Lakers jerseys in the crowd as Nuggets gear. Still, as Denver's teams have found success and the city itself has grown, local support has increased dramatically. These days, it's tough to get a ticket to a Nuggets or a Colorado Avalanche game.

The one outlier in all of this is the Colorado Rockies. As of this writing, Coors Field is thirty-one years old, and while the Rockies have had a few good seasons—even making it to the World Series once—they've been downright awful lately. Despite that, they still draw impressive crowds. That's just another reason why Denver is a great sports town.

Did I block Dr. J? Of course not. (Photograph courtesy of the Denver Public Library, Western History Collection, call # RMN-026-5346.)

I don't remember the exact year, but early in my time playing in Denver I had a solid game one night. The next day, a sports reporter wrote that I played like a Thoroughbred. The day after that, Bob King, the executive vice president of the Nuggets, came into the locker room after practice. In front of everyone, he said, "I read you played like a Thoroughbred." Then he added, "I thought you played more like a Clydesdale."

Everyone knew about my love for Thoroughbreds because I was always carrying a racing form, a copy of *BloodHorse* magazine, or something related to horse racing. So, after Bob's comment, my teammates started calling me "The Horse," and the nickname stuck. It's fitting, I think, not only because it reflected my passion for the Thoroughbred industry, but also because it symbolized my consistency as a basketball player. Over my fifteen years in professional basketball, I only missed twenty-four games, so I was always there when the team needed me. But my consistency as a player would soon be tested in ways I hadn't anticipated.

Around the time of Scott's birth, our family faced a crisis that changed my perspective on professional basketball. My brother, Greg, and his wife, Paula, had moved to Lexington, where Greg worked for my horseman friend Tom Gentry. Unfortunately, Greg contracted a virus that led to reduced kidney function. His condition worsened to the point where he met the criteria for a kidney transplant at just twenty-nine years old. Greg and Paula decided to move back to Batavia, where he began dialysis and they could receive support from my parents as well as other relatives and friends in the area.

Back then, kidney transplant surgeries were less successful due to organ rejection. The transplant surgeon they consulted told Greg that he would only perform the procedure if the donor kidney came from an immediate family member. This meant that my parents, Kathi, and I had to undergo special blood testing to see if one of us was a match. My dad, who was fifty-four years old, turned out to be the best donor because of his blood type and other factors.

Surgeons performed Greg's transplant surgery at Rush Hospital in Chicago on January 14, 1981. The Nuggets had a game in Phoenix that day, so afterward I took a red-eye flight to Chicago and went straight to the hospital. When I arrived, I was amazed to find Greg sitting up in a wheelchair, a big smile on his face. He had received one of my dad's kidneys and was doing fine. My dad, the donor, underwent a more difficult operation due to the medical limitations at the time, and he was out of

Grandpa Meyer was a major influence in my life and one of my biggest supporters.

it for about twenty-four hours. In fact, the first person he responded to was a hospital volunteer, who opened the door to his room and, unaware of my dad's condition, cheerily announced, "Craft cart!"

Without missing a beat, my dad replied, "Crap cart? We've got enough crap in here," and drifted back to sleep.

Our family gathered in prayer to give thanks for the success of the transplant. Afterward, Greg had to take several medications, including antirejection drugs. Both of them recovered so well that Dad was able to return to his contract painting business, with Greg joining him.

While Greg endured his pre- and posttransplant ordeal, my life with the Nuggets continued to bring its own set of surprises. In August of 1978, the Nuggets traded Bobby Jones to the Philadelphia 76ers for George McGinnis, which I found unbelievable. Don't get me wrong—George was one of the best NBA players in his prime. But by this time his production had started to decline, and so had his physical condition. For example, during our training camp at the Air Force Academy, which sits at over seven thousand feet of elevation, Larry Brown had us running a three-line fast break up and down the court. There were about eighteen of us, so each player rotated into the drill every sixth time. But George was just walking around, seemingly without a care in the world, and only joining in every tenth or twelfth turn. Furious, Larry blew his whistle and barked, "Everybody back to the locker room!" Once inside, he gave a speech, saying we weren't there to clown around—we were there to work. We all knew he was talking about George. Then Larry said, "Now get back out there and take your turn in the three lines." He called Carl Scheer by phone and said, "Get George out of here." George had been a Nugget for only about ten minutes, and Larry already wanted to trade him.

To make matters worse, our star shooting guard, David Thompson, was beginning to decline due to his drug use. As a result, we finished fourth in the Western Conference with a record of 47–35 and lost to the Lakers in the first round of the postseason playoffs. Larry Brown left to coach at UCLA, and Doug Moe stepped into the head coaching role.

Midway through the 1979–80 season, the Nuggets traded George McGinnis for Alex English, which turned out to be one of the best trades in the franchise's history. Alex became the highest-scoring NBA player of the 1980s, accumulating over twenty-one thousand points. So, the best trade we ever made—and the worst—both involved George McGinnis. There wasn't anyone who could stop Alex one-on-one. He had a jump shot that he released way out in front of his body, making him impossible to defend, especially with Doug Moe's coaching style. We played a passing game, with no real set plays to speak of. You passed the ball, and you had three options: set a screen, cut toward the basket, or cut away from it. It was constant motion. Because of that, it was very difficult to double-team anyone.

Our team needed a boost to the roster, and prior to the 1980 NBA draft our assistant coach, George Irvine, told me the Nuggets were keen on Kevin McHale, a power forward from the University of Minnesota. The Boston Celtics had the number one pick that year and could have acquired Joe Barry Carroll, a center from Purdue University who was considered the best college player available. Instead, the Celtics dealt their number one draft pick to the Golden State Warriors for Robert Parish and another Warriors first-round pick, which they used to draft McHale. So, the Warriors wound up with Carroll, who never quite lived up to expectations, while the Celtics ended up with two players who would form one of the best front lines in NBA history alongside Larry Bird.

As for the Nuggets, we didn't have much money, so we didn't do extensive college scouting. If you look at our draft picks from that time, they were mostly players from the University of North Carolina (UNC) or players who had competed against UNC. When we reached the fifth pick in 1980, we selected James Ray from Jacksonville University. I got a phone call from Mike Pratt, who was the head coach at UNC Charlotte at the time. "What in the world are you doing drafting James Ray?" Mike asked. "He's not the fifth-best player in our conference, let alone the fifth-best player in the country." Ray turned out to be a bust as the fifth pick in the draft, but a few months into the season we acquired former UCLA star forward Kiki VanDeWeghe in a roundabout way. Kiki's father, Ernie, was a physician who had played for the New York Knicks and still had family in the area, so he fully expected Kiki to be selected by the Knicks as the twelfth pick. Instead, the Dallas Mavericks chose Kiki as the eleventh pick, but Kiki refused to play for them and demanded a trade.

In December of 1980, we acquired Kiki from Dallas in exchange for two first-round draft picks: one in 1981 and the other in 1986. From that moment on, things started to turn around. With a front line of Alex, Kiki, and myself, we weren't exactly defensive stalwarts, so we had to score a lot of points to win. And score we did; we won a lot of games with that lineup on the floor.

During our downtime on the road, we found creative ways to pass the time. On commercial airline flights, four or five of us often played Tonk, a card game similar to five-card gin rummy. We played with actual cash, at $5 or $10 a hand, and four or five of us would be sitting in first class with a $100 pot spread out in the aisle. But the flight attendants (and sometimes other passengers in first class) didn't think that was a good look. Eventually we started to keep score on a piece of paper instead. Still, there were times on commercial flights when you'd see $75 or $100 just lying on the floor in first class.

Pranks were a common occurrence, especially ones I cooked up with my teammates Kim Hughes and Glen Gondrezick. For example, we used to get a rooming list whenever we went on the road. Chopper would hand it out so everyone knew exactly which room each person was in.

Back then, hotels had these door hangers you could use to order breakfast—just fill it out and hang it on your door the night before, and room service would deliver your breakfast at the time you requested. I haven't seen those in a while, but they were common then. So, whether

In-game action vs. the Nets with Hall of Famer David Thompson (33), who was the most talented teammate I ever played with. (Photograph courtesy of the Denver Public Library, Western History Collection, call # RMN-056-6619.)

it was a media member we didn't particularly like or a rookie, we'd have some fun. We'd fill out one of those hangers with a huge breakfast order, set the earliest delivery time possible, like 6:30 in the morning, and hang it on their door after they went to sleep. Sure enough, they'd get a knock at the crack of dawn with a full breakfast they didn't ask for.

Another favorite prank was having the hotel operator call a rookie's room to say that shootaround had been moved up, telling them to be in the lobby at 10 a.m. instead of 11. So, there they'd be, standing around an hour early, completely alone. We never played these pranks on fellow veterans, just rookies or sometimes the media folks traveling with us.

I don't recall being on the receiving end of any pranks during my rookie year, but I did have to lug around a medical ultrasound machine during road trips with the Colonels. That thing was huge, about the size of a five-gallon bucket. Even though I was leading the league in scoring, I still had to carry that big machine everywhere we went!

At the end of nearly every NBA season, my family and I would pack up the car and drive to Kentucky for the summer. We had a houseboat on Herrington Lake, which became our frequent getaway spot. In fact, the summer Cheri was pregnant with Scott, we spent almost the entire season on that houseboat. It had air conditioning and cable television, so we were comfortable. Every Saturday around noon, when the lake traffic picked up, we'd pack up and head to Cheri's parents' house to do laundry, grocery shop, spend the night, attend church on Sunday, and return to the houseboat as most people were leaving. As Sheridan and Scott got older and became more involved in activities in Denver, our time spent in Kentucky grew shorter. But we have many great memories from those trips.

While those summers in Kentucky offered a welcome escape from the grind of the NBA season, life on the road with the Nuggets came with its own set of unforgettable stories. We had played a game in Detroit on December 23, 1982, while Cheri and the kids were in Lexington. On the morning of the 24th, I flew from Detroit to Lexington to spend Christmas Eve with them. That same morning, the team left Detroit en route to Denver but only made it as far as Chicago. Denver had been hit by one of the biggest snowstorms in its history, forcing the airport to shut down for thirty-three hours.[1] Some areas got over three feet of snow, and the airport itself received more than two feet. The team checked into the O'Hare Marriott to wait it out.

When I heard about the situation, my family and I managed to catch a flight from Lexington to Chicago later that afternoon. Considering the snowstorm, I knew we could get to Denver much more quickly from Chicago than from the smaller airport in Lexington. So, on Christmas Day 1982, we all found ourselves at the Marriott Chicago O'Hare—me, Cheri, Scott, Sheridan, the entire team, the coaches, and our trainer, Robert "Chopper" Travaglini. It felt like we were the only people in the whole hotel. I still remember a couple of my teammates playing in the lobby with Scott and his remote-controlled car. I felt a little guilty because, out of everyone on the team, I was the only one who got to spend Christmas with my family—even if it was in the O'Hare Marriott.

On the morning of the 26th, Chopper got us on a flight to Denver, which was still buried under more than two feet of snow. He arranged for a bus to take us straight to McNichols Arena. After all the delays, we finally made it home.

During my nine years with the Nuggets, the person I spent the most time with was Chopper Travaglini. A New Jersey native, he attended Niagara University for one semester before flunking out. He later became a

The most successful horse I ever owned with Tom Gentry was Secretarial Queen, a mare who was part of Secretariat's first crop. Here she is winning a stakes race at Hollywood Park in 1980.

trainer for the Philadelphia Bulldogs in the Continental Football League. Although Chopper had no formal training, he became an exceptional trainer through trial and error. He could diagnose injuries before you even got an X-ray or saw a doctor—he was that good.

Before joining the Nuggets in 1979, Chopper was the trainer for the Virginia Squires. He was also a gambler, and honestly he would have been a perfect fit for *The Sopranos.* He was a three-pack-a-day smoker, spoke with a raspy voice, and lived in a hotel room at the Holiday Inn right next to McNichols Arena. Chopper was the only person I knew who, at any given time, had his entire net worth in his front pocket. He would trade his Nuggets season tickets with the hotel manager for his room. His wardrobe—comprised of alpaca sweaters and polyester slacks—said it all. The only money he spent was on food and gambling.

On the road we were inseparable. We spent our off days at racetracks, but Chopper knew everyone. When my son, Scott, was about four or five years old, he loved watching wrestling on television. One night, Chopper, Scott, and I attended a wrestling event at Denver Auditorium Arena, where Andre the Giant was the headliner. After the event, we tried to go backstage, but security wouldn't let Scott in because of his age. Undeterred, Chopper went straight into the locker room, got Andre the Giant, and brought him out so Scott could meet him. Chopper knew *everyone*!

One time, I was on the phone with my brother, Greg, in Chopper's office when the Cubs had made it to the 1984 National League Championship Series. They were set to face the San Diego Padres, and game one was at Wrigley Field. Greg asked me, "Do you know anyone who can get me tickets to the Cubs-Padres game? I've tried everyone I know, and I can't find any." Chopper overheard our conversation and told me to hang up the phone. So, I told Greg, "Chopper must need the phone. I'll call you back." After hanging up, Chopper dialed Jack McKeon, the general manager of the San Diego Padres at the time. They had met when Jack was with the Tidewater Tides, a Triple-A team that later became the Norfolk Tides in Virginia. Chopper said, "Jack, I need two tickets to the first game in Chicago." As a result, Greg ended up meeting Jack McKeon in his hotel room in Chicago and got two tickets to the game!

After Chopper retired from the Nuggets, he became president of the Denver Nuggets Community Fund. In the late 1980s, he founded "Chopper's Dinner," which has since become the largest fundraiser for both the Nuggets and the Colorado Avalanche.[2] The annual event raises over $200,000 each year for local children's charities. Chopper passed away in 1999, but his legacy lives on through that event. Additionally, the street that Ball Arena is located on is named Chopper Circle in his honor.

Chopper's impact on the Denver community was undeniable, and his legacy remains embedded in the fabric of the Nuggets organization. Similarly, as I reflect on my career, I'm reminded of the influence that certain people had on my growth as a player, particularly the matchups I faced against some of the game's greatest talents. Kareem was the best player I ever faced. I had some success against him, and in fact Kareem once reportedly said that I was one of the toughest players for him to guard in the NBA. I always respected him. However, the player I truly struggled with was Moses Malone. Moses was a few inches taller than me, but he also had incredible quickness. The advantage I had against most NBA centers was that they weren't accustomed to coming out of the post to guard someone. Most centers played primarily in the low post. But Moses had the agility to step out on the floor and defend me. While Moses Malone was the toughest opponent I played against, Kareem was the best.

I had sixty-two head-to-head matchups with Kareem, who I believe was the greatest center to ever play the game. (Photograph courtesy of the Denver Public Library, Western History Collection, call # RMN-056-6596.)

Two other NBA greats, Earvin "Magic" Johnson and Larry Bird, were key to improving the popularity of the league. They first squared off in the NCAA championship game back in 1979. Larry, nicknamed "the Hick from French Lick," played for the Indiana State Sycamores, an underdog team, while Magic starred for the Michigan State Spartans. That matchup really captivated the country: the Hick from French Lick vs. the polished star from a big program. It became the highest-rated NCAA championship game in history.[3] Michigan State won the game, 75–64.

From there, both players went on to transform the NBA. At the time, the league still required players to be four years removed from high school before entering the draft. But because Bird had taken a year off before enrolling at Indiana State, he was eligible to be drafted after his junior year.

The Celtics took a gamble, drafting him in 1978 and waiting a year while he finished his senior season. Whether they thought they could lure him into turning pro early or just believed in his talent enough to wait, it paid off. When he finally joined Boston in 1979, he made an immediate impact and earned rookie of the year honors.

In 1980, the Celtics pulled off one of the most lopsided trades in NBA history, trading the number one pick, Joe Barry Carroll, to the Golden State Warriors for Robert Parish and the third overall pick, which they used to draft Kevin McHale. Suddenly, Bird was playing alongside one of the best front lines the NBA has ever seen.

Bird and Magic were both players who truly made everyone around them better. It's a cliché, but in their case it was absolutely true. Bird, in particular, was the ultimate team player. The Celtics had Dennis Johnson, one of the best defensive guards of that era, and Danny Ainge was also on those teams. But Bird's unselfishness elevated everyone. Boston went on to win three championships during that era: 1981, 1984, and 1986.

As for my relationship with Larry, we never had much of a personal connection. I heard he once told someone he came to a Colonels game and I refused to sign an autograph for him. And, as I've said before, aside from the night Sheridan was born, I can't recall many times I didn't stay after games to sign autographs. But if that happened, I understand why he might not have held me in high regard.

Bird was also one of the great trash talkers—not loud or showy, but always talking. He'd say things like "You can't guard me" or "What do you think you're doing?" One of my favorite stories is from the first-ever NBA three-point contest. He supposedly walked into the locker room and asked, "So, who's finishing second tonight?" And then, of course, he went out and won the whole thing. He could back it up, every time. He's absolutely in the conversation for the greatest small forward of all time.

As for Magic, he was the number one overall pick in the 1979 NBA draft. Bird had been the sixth pick the year before. The Lakers ended up with Magic as the top pick in 1979 because of a series of planned trades and decisions dating back to 1976. Kareem had already been in Los Angeles for six or seven years and hadn't won a championship. After Magic arrived, the Lakers started piling them up.

Magic was a joy to be around—always smiling, always upbeat. He'd ask, "How's everything?" or "You doing okay?" Just a terrific personality. That college rivalry between Magic and Bird carried over to the NBA for nearly a decade. It seemed like every year it was either the Lakers with Magic and Kareem or the Celtics with Bird winning the title.

Around that time, Commissioner David Stern made a brilliant move by shifting the NBA's marketing focus toward individual stars rather than teams. That decision—combined with the star power of Bird, Magic, and, later, Michael Jordan—was crucial in turning the NBA into the global phenomenon it is today. People sometimes ask me what I think about Jordan. While Magic and Larry Bird were instrumental in revitalizing the NBA, I believe Michael Jordan had an even greater impact than either of them.

I have a recording of one of my last games at Chicago Stadium, where the Bulls used to play. Competing in there was always special to me, since the arena was about forty miles from where I grew up. That meant a lot of family and friends would come out and watch. In the video, I'm at the free-throw line with a camera under the basket capturing my face. And I remember clearly: at the far end of the arena, there wasn't a single person seated. That was during the 1984–85 season—Michael's rookie year—and back then Chicago Stadium was still half empty for games. But as his career progressed, he became must-watch basketball, and demand for Bulls tickets increased dramatically. I give him as much credit as anyone for pulling the NBA out of the so-called Dark Ages. He was just that captivating.

To me, Michael Jordan is the greatest player in NBA history. Look at his rookie year. He came in and averaged around twenty-eight points per game. Offensively, he was phenomenal, no question. But what truly set him apart was his defense. He was named to the NBA All-Defensive First Team nine times during his career and was named Defensive Player of the Year in 1988.

But what I admire most was his competitiveness. Sure, he had a few injuries, but when he was healthy, he played every night. No load management, no skipping back-to-backs. He just showed up and competed, every single game. That kind of consistency and drive is rare. I've heard stories about how intense he was in practice, too. That's a coach's dream. When your best player also practices the hardest, it sets the tone for everyone else.

Look out below! Dunking against the Buffalo Braves.

Thinking about that kind of relentless commitment made me reflect on my own career and how I wanted to finish it. Before the start of the 1984–85 NBA season, I announced that it would be my final year. When I began my professional basketball career, I had no idea it would last fifteen years. Honestly, I never expected it to go that long. But my biggest concern was not overstaying my usefulness. I'd seen too many athletes stick around past their prime, and I always felt it diminished their legacy. I didn't want to be one of them.

Prior to my final season with the Nuggets, we made a major trade: Kiki VanDeWeghe for what felt like half the Portland Trail Blazers' roster. One of the players we got in return was Wayne Cooper. When the 1984–85 season began, I started coming off the bench for the first time since junior high school. It was a difficult adjustment.

By the end of the year, I was playing more and more, but I had already decided: I didn't want to be a bench player. Physically, I probably could have played a couple more years, but mentally it wore on me. There were nights I'd drive to the arena and wonder why I was still doing it. So, when I announced it would be my last year and that I was retiring, I felt a huge sense of relief. Ironically, I played better in the second half of that season than I had in the first.

Looking back, I truly believe I retired at the right time. I might have had more basketball left in me physically, but for all the other reasons, it was time to move on. One example I often think of is Willie Mays. After his legendary career with the Giants—first in New York and then in San Francisco—he played one final season with the Mets. I remember seeing him misjudge a fly ball in center field, and it dropped over his head. I hated watching that. A great player struggling like that; it stayed with me. I never wanted to be in that position.

The truth is, I was always motivated more by a fear of failure than by any expectation of success. That mindset came directly from my speech teacher at Batavia High, Pat Scanlon, whom I mentioned earlier in the book. When she warned me that I might not be able to play college basketball unless I took my grades seriously, it made a lasting impression. It stayed with me for life. But when fear is what drives you, that anxiety grows as your performance dips. It becomes harder to manage, because you're constantly battling the sense that you're falling short. That fear of failure drove me; it helped shape who I became, both on and off the court.

Once word got out that "The Horse" was retiring, I received some nice recognition throughout the league. The San Antonio Spurs gave me a pair of boots, the Utah Jazz presented me with a rocking chair, the Los Angeles Clippers gifted Cheri and me a trip to Hawaii, and the Denver Nuggets handed me the keys to a Ford F-150 pickup, which I later used on our farm in Kentucky. Our team reached the Western Conference Finals, where we faced the Lakers and their "Showtime" roster, which included

Kareem, Magic Johnson, James Worthy, and Michael Cooper. We didn't stand much of a chance, but we did manage to win game two of the series. In the decisive game five on May 22, the Lakers were ahead by more than forty points. Cheri attended that game, but the kids stayed home. With about three minutes left in the game, I was sitting at the end of the bench, reflecting on this being my last game as a professional player. Then I heard Doug Moe call my name. For a moment I thought I was imagining it and wondered, "Why is he calling me?" Doug called my name again, so I got up and walked toward him courtside. He looked at me and said, "I want your last shot to be a three-pointer."

After I checked into the game, Kurt Rambis was guarding me. The first time down the court, he was right up on me, and I had no chance to shoot. The second time down, I got a wide-open look at a three-pointer. I wasn't much of a three-point shooter, but I let it fly, and by the grace of God it went in. So, my last shot as a professional player was a three-pointer at The Forum against the Lakers. I was even on the Lakers' "Star of the Game" show with Chick Hearn, despite us losing by forty-four points. I had a good relationship with Chick because he was from the Fox River Valley, the same place I was from. They gave me the game ball, and I took it home and gave it to Scott, saying, "This is the ball that Dad made his last three-point shot with." Since the ball had the Los Angeles Lakers logo on it, Scott took it, looked at it, and said, "You mean Kareem and Magic touched this ball?" That's where I stood with him!

From the first day I played professional basketball, my dream was always to return to Central Kentucky and have our own horse farm. That's what I saved for and educated myself about. I subscribed to *BloodHorse* magazine and had a set of tapes on horse farm management and how to assess a horse's conformation. That was my dream, and I was fully prepared for it. I played fifteen years of professional basketball and squeezed everything I possibly could out of it. Physically, I could have played some more, but mentally I was ready for it to be over. I was satisfied. What I did miss, though, was the camaraderie of the locker room. With twelve players, a handful of coaches, and a trainer, you're all in it together, trying to accomplish the same things. That's what I missed the most. I finished my career at age thirty-six, averaging 22.9 points, 9.1 rebounds, and 2.4 assists per game, and as of this writing I am the third-leading all-time scorer in Nuggets history, having scored 16,589 points during my time with the franchise. (Alex English holds the Nuggets scoring title with 21,645 points.) In an article about my retirement, *Los Angeles Times* reporter Sam McManis asked me to reflect on my career. "I got a good salary but I never shortchanged anybody," I told him. "Not the fans, not the man who signed my paycheck. I gave it everything I had." I can live with that.[4]

I closed out my career being honored with the NBA J. Walter Kennedy Citizenship Award, an honor presented annually by the Professional Basketball Writers Association to a player, coach, or athletic trainer who demonstrates exceptional service and dedication to the community. Named after the NBA's second commissioner, the award was a meaningful recognition of the work I tried to do off the court with organizations in Denver and in Greater Colorado, such as the Alzheimer's Association, the American Cancer Society, the American Heart Association, the National Kidney Foundation, and Gathering Place, a shelter for homeless women and children.

Even after my time in the NBA, Cheri and I remained committed to giving back. In 2008, she and I organized a live auction package for a three-day trip to New York City to watch the Belmont Stakes, with proceeds benefiting the American Cancer Society. It was a trip for four, with Cheri and I hosting. The winning bidders were Susan and Kent Vick of Denver.

Coincidentally, one of Susan's close friends was Barbara Goldy. So, after Susan won the auction, the Vicks, the Goldys, Cheri, and I all went to New York together. We kicked off the weekend with a Friday lunch before the Saturday races and had a fantastic time—dined at some great restaurants, took a boat tour around Manhattan, and spent Saturday afternoon at Belmont Park. During Friday's lunch, I pulled out the *Daily Racing Form* and gave everyone a quick handicapping lesson. Then I added, "Now tomorrow at the races, don't bother me with any questions."

That year, Big Brown was going for the Triple Crown. Unfortunately, he didn't win—in fact, he didn't even finish the race. He was eased before the wire. Still, it was a memorable experience and we raised $15,000 for the American Cancer Society.

There were some funny moments, too. For instance, I only drink Budweiser beer. One of the restaurants we visited didn't carry it. Barbara, who is not exactly a shy New Yorker, told the server, "There's a deli next door. Go buy a six-pack." And that's exactly what they did. They served it to me in a glass so no one would notice I was drinking Budweiser. Apparently, the place thought they were too upscale for it. But that's what I drank, and I loved it.

From left: Kent and Susan Vick, buyers of the American Cancer Society charity trip, with Bill and Barbara Goldy, and Cheri and me at Belmont Park.

Another unforgettable moment came in 1985, when the Denver Nuggets retired my number 44 jersey. It was an incredible honor and the perfect way to wrap up my career.

I'd like to take a moment to reflect on some of the referees I've worked with over the years. When I first broke into the ABA, officials were different. You could actually talk to them. They didn't have egos, at least not the kind that made them think they never made mistakes.

Early on, the ABA was always trying to figure out how to be a thorn in the NBA's side. One of the things they did was hire away four of the NBA's top officials: Norm Drucker, Earl Strom, Joe Gushue, and John Vanak. I liked all four of them because you could have a real conversation with them on the court.

One of my favorites was Earl Strom, a tough guy who grew up near Philly. You could say something like, "Earl, you missed that one," and he'd reply, "Maybe you're right. Maybe I did." When an official says that, there's not much more you can argue. One time, Earl was officiating a game at the Commonwealth Convention Center in Louisville. During a timeout, a fan was giving him absolute hell—yelling, swearing, the whole deal. Earl told him to knock it off. But during the next timeout, the guy kept going. I guess Earl figured security wasn't going to handle it, so he went up into the stands and got into a fight with the fan right there on the spot!

Another ref I really liked was Jess Kersey, an ABA ref who came over to the NBA after the merger. One time, he was refereeing a Pacers game, and George McGinnis came running up from behind and plowed right over him. George said it was an accident. I don't think Jess believed him, and George got a small fine and a suspension. Later, in another game with Jess officiating, I was running down the court close to him and said, "Jess, watch out—McGinnis is behind you." Jess almost swallowed his whistle from laughing so hard.

Personally, I always had a good relationship with the officials. In fifteen years of playing professional basketball, I was only ejected once: at Madison Square Garden in a game against the Knicks, just before Christmas near the end of my career. Cheri and the kids were at that game. I was going up for a rebound with my elbows out when I got shoved from behind. Paul Westphal was trying to box me out, and my elbow went up and over his head. Hue Hollins was one of the officials, and all he saw was my elbow flying by Paul's head. He thought I was throwing it at him and tossed me from the game. At the time, my son, Scott, was just a little guy, and he was afraid they were going to arrest me and take me to jail! Later, I received a letter from NBA Commissioner David Stern. After league officials reviewed the tape of the incident, he rescinded the fine and apologized for Hue's call. From time to time after that, I'd remind Hue I had a letter from the commissioner saying he blew the call.

Years later, when I became a coach, my relationship with refs grew more contentious. I was ejected from several games, but only once did I feel it wasn't deserved. During my first stint as the Nuggets coach, we hosted a Sunday afternoon game that Cheri, my son, Scott, and his first date attended. Jake O'Donnell was one of the refs that day. I don't know if he thought I said something or what exactly happened, but he threw me out of the game in the first half. After getting tossed, I took off my coat and threw it on the floor. Later that evening we went out to dinner as planned, then dropped Scott's date off on the way home. After we dropped her off, Scott turned to me and said, "I'm never bringing another girl to a Nuggets game again." I think I embarrassed myself, him, and probably the whole family, but that was the only time something like that happened.

In my view, there are three reasons a coach might get thrown out of a game. First, you hope it might swing the officiating your way. It doesn't. Second, you're trying to fire up your team, but that rarely works, either. And third, your team is playing so poorly that you just want an excuse to get to the locker room early. That one's pretty common.

My favorite referee when I coached in the NBA was Dick Bavetta. He was one of those officials you could actually talk to—just a great, funny guy. He was inducted into the Naismith Memorial Basketball Hall of Fame in 2015, the same year as Louie Dampier and John Calipari. I've never seen anyone more genuinely appreciative of being inducted into the Hall of Fame than Dick.

Later in my coaching career, though, things changed. The officials became almost impossible to talk to. Their egos just wouldn't allow them to admit, "Yeah, I might've missed that call." I never heard that kind of honesty from refs later on. One official in particular, Steve Javie, seemed to have it out for me. Almost every time he officiated one of our games, either I'd get a technical or Nick Van Exel would. Our relationship got so bad that the NBA actually asked the two of us to sit down and talk. One day after shootaround at the Staples Center, we met in a conference room—me, Steve, Denny McGowan (our assistant general manager), and an NBA representative. I brought the Lakers' scouting report with me and laid it on the table. It was a couple of pages long.

Steve and I had a very honest, direct conversation. I told him I thought he was biased against me and the Nuggets, which was why we always seemed to get so many technical fouls when he officiated. He told me that wasn't true, and that *he* thought *I* had it out for *him*. We shook hands, and things were better after that. But as we were wrapping up, Steve pointed to the scouting report and said, "Is that all?"

I said, "Yeah, that's all I've got to say."

He looked at the pages and said, "I thought those were all the issues you wanted to bring up; it looked like two pages' worth!"

We both laughed, and our relationship was better from that time on.

While my experiences with referees had their own dynamics, my interactions with other coaches were almost nonexistent. One thing that surprised me about the coaching fraternity was how distant it felt, at least in my experience as a head coach. I remember one time I called Rudy Tomjanovich after he won the first of two consecutive championships with the Houston Rockets in 1994. Rudy and I weren't close, but we did share a connection in that our very first college games were against each other. That was in 1968, when the Wildcats traveled to Ann Arbor to play Michigan in their then-new arena. I left a voicemail for Rudy congratulating him on the championship but I never heard back.

When I look at some of the great coaches I went up against, I'd have to put Phil Jackson at the top of the list. The fact that he won eleven championships with two different teams is phenomenal. You can argue that he had great talent with Michael Jordan and Scottie Pippen in Chicago and then Kobe and Shaq in Los Angeles with the Lakers, but having the best team doesn't always guarantee you a championship title.

Another fellow coach I admired was Gregg Popovich, whom I've known for a long time. I first met Pop when I was a player and we had training camp at the Air Force Academy, where he was an assistant coach. Later on, Larry Brown hired him to be an assistant at San Antonio. In 1996, four years after Larry was fired by the Spurs, Popovich was named head coach and led the franchise to five NBA championships.

I also had great respect for Pat Riley, even though we weren't particularly close. You could easily make the case that the Lakers teams he coached during their "Showtime" era, with future Hall of Famers Kareem Abdul-Jabbar, Magic Johnson, and James Worthy, were among the greatest NBA teams of all time. Of course, Pat later left to coach the New York Knicks and the Miami Heat, where he won another championship with a talented group of players.

What has always amazed me about coaching is how difficult it is to excel at both the college and pro levels. Many legendary college coaches in the Hall of Fame struggled when they jumped to the NBA, including Jerry Tarkanian, Rick Pitino, and John Calipari. A notable exception is Larry Brown, who found success in both. Similarly, it's difficult for a great pro player to become a great pro coach. One exception is Lenny Wilkins, who earned induction into the Hall of Fame as both a player and coach, an achievement I admire.

The coach I admire most is Larry Brown. He was an All-Star guard in the ABA before becoming a successful coach in college and in the NBA. He led the Kansas Jayhawks to the 1988 NCAA championship and the Detroit Pistons to the 2004 NBA championship. He didn't stay in one place too long, but he found success everywhere he went. I had the pleasure of playing for Larry with the Nuggets early in my tenure. He was an outstanding coach at every level. I also say that about Hubie Brown.

I give Hubie most of the credit for our 1975 Kentucky Colonels ABA championship, because we'd had the same cast of characters and hadn't been able to win a championship until Hubie got there.

Another coach that I developed a good relationship with was Don Nelson. Don was always very supportive, always giving advice. In fact, one time early in my coaching tenure he was coaching the Golden State Warriors. We met in the hallway after the game and he asked, "What are you doing for dinner?"

I said, "I don't know. I'll go out and have dinner someplace."

He said, "Come on and go with me." We went to a really nice Italian place close to the coliseum in Oakland and talked basketball for a couple of hours. I always appreciated Don. He was the most helpful coach I had during my coaching career.

One thing's for sure: I don't miss wearing suits and sportscoats on the sidelines, which was the standard during my coaching days. I've never liked shopping for clothes. And now that I'm retired, my wardrobe, which was never a priority to begin with, matters even less.

Cheri always teases me about my shirts. She says I don't own one that doesn't have a logo on it. I've got plenty of Batavia basketball gear that they still send me regularly, a bunch of UK shirts, and even several Kansas T-shirts from my trip to Lawrence in February of 2023. Visiting Allen Fieldhouse had always been on my bucket list, so I attended a home game against the West Virginia Mountaineers with Bill and Barbara Goldy's granddaughter, Morgan, who was a student there at the time. I had met Kansas coach Bill Self on several previous occasions, and he offered us seats behind the Kansas bench, right next to former Jayhawk standout Roger Morningstar. They showed me on national television sitting behind the bench wearing a Kansas T-shirt. I caught grief from some Kentucky fans for that!

Funny story. One of the first times I met Bill Self was in 2008, soon after the college basketball season ended. I was at Keeneland and ran into then–UK coach Billy Gillispie.

"Are you going to the Derby?" he asked.

I said, "No, we don't have tickets this year."

He replied, "Well, come and go with me." Then he asked, "How many of you are there?"

I said, "It'd be me, Cheri, Scott, and Sheridan."

I assume Billy was gifted the tickets. I can't imagine he bought them himself. He had been given two eight-seat boxes at Churchill Downs for the Derby. We attended with Billy, a couple of his assistant coaches and their wives, and several other coaches he had worked with over the years, including Bill Self, who had once been his boss at the University of Illinois. At one point during the day, Bill went to a concession stand, bought a whole tray of tacos, and brought them back to the boxes for everyone. Nice gesture. And from a Jayhawk, no less.

8

Courtland Dreams, Cut Short

By the time I retired, Cheri and I had bought a horse farm in Versailles and named it Courtland. We decided to put our house on the market in January 1985, thinking it would take a while to sell. However, we sold it quickly and had to move out in about thirty days. We rented a two-bedroom suite at a Sheraton Hotel near our old house. The hotel's assistant general manager was Barbara Goldy, whose husband, Bill, had played basketball and baseball at St. John's and had spent time in the minor leagues. Cheri knew Barbara through some charity work she'd been involved with. Barbara allowed us to rent the suite and even let us bring our two dogs, despite the Sheraton's usual no-pet policy. The Goldys are still our best friends in Denver to this day. We stayed in that suite until the playoffs were over, and then we moved to Courtland. The only downside was that Sheridan (who would have been about thirteen at the time) and Scott learned how to order room service, which made our bill astronomical at the end of each month.

Once we arrived in Versailles, my basketball career was in the rear-view mirror and I was immersed in living my dream of getting Courtland up and running. We planted trees, built fences, blacktopped roads, and bought horses. The goal was to breed mares and sell the yearlings at the annual Keeneland September Yearling Sale. We had some great success, selling one yearling for $725,000 and another for $450,000. At that time, you really had to be careless to fail in the horse business.

Our first Christmas card at Courtland Farm in Versailles, Kentucky.

One reason I love the Thoroughbred industry so much is because I see a strong parallel between horse racing and human athletics. You can have a horse with exceptional breeding and perfect conformation, yet it still might not outrun you or me simply because it lacks heart.

In the world of buying and selling horses, no one has figured out how to measure that intangible quality: how much try a horse has. And I think the same principle applies to human athletes. You'll see people with all the talent and physical tools in the world, but if they don't have the heart and the drive to be great, no amount of coaching can give them that.

That's one of the enduring mysteries of both human athletics and the Thoroughbred industry: no one has yet figured out how to predict who truly has the heart, the ambition, and the will to compete, whether it's a horse or a human.

Shortly after we moved to the farm, we received a visit from Wayne Smith, a longtime friend of Cheri's parents. He was the minister at Southland Christian Church, a large congregation in Lexington. He invited us to attend Southland, but we told him we wanted to be more involved in our local community, so we started to attend Woodford Christian Church in Versailles. Their minister at the time was Gary Black, who became a good friend.

With my high school coaches, Bob Abbott (*left*) and Don Vandersnick, at Dan Issel Day in Batavia, 1985.

I remember our first service there. After it ended, while Gary was still at the pulpit, he acknowledged me and my family and said, "Now, don't you kids all run back there and get his offering—I mean autograph." That broke up the whole congregation in laughter.

Our family became very involved with Woodford Christian, so much so that we hosted church dinners and meetings at our farm. It became a kind of gathering place for various church activities. Our kids joined the youth group as well, and our son, Scott, became close friends with Gary and Linda Black's son, John, who was the same age.

One summer we hosted a church picnic at the farm. We set up a big tent and about two hundred people attended. I even hired a helicopter to give guests short rides around Versailles. I remember one guest: an eighty-year-old woman who had never been in an airplane before, let alone a helicopter. She went up in the helicopter for her first flying experience, and it was really special.

Signing an autograph for Corey Williams on Dan Issel Day in Batavia. Ironically, Corey would later break my scoring record at Batavia High School.

Living in Versailles also gave us meaningful time to spend with Cheri's mom and dad, as well as with her sister, Vicki—something we appreciated after spending ten years in Denver.

In the fall of 1985, Cheri and I traveled with my family to my hometown of Batavia, where the city honored my retirement from basketball with a celebration called "Dan Issel Day." The celebration included a reception and a short ceremony held in the very gym where I had once played. By then, it had become Batavia Junior High. Coach Van, Assistant Coach Bob Abbott, and some of my teammates attended, and longtime Batavia mayor Jeff Schielke offered remarks. During an autograph session, I signed something for a young Corey Williams, who would later break my scoring record at Batavia and go on to play for the other Wildcats: the team in Arizona.

It was a special event. I truly appreciated the city of Batavia recognizing me in such a meaningful way. Back in the Bluegrass State, as we settled into our new routines, the horse business was starting to heat up.

The prices in the mid-1980s were unbelievable. One of my favorite stories from that time involves a bloodstock agent named Paula Cline. She knew I was looking to buy broodmares, so one day she called me up and said, "I've got this mare that I think you might be interested in." The sellers were asking $250,000. I was busy at the time, so I asked a young vet named Kirk Shiner and my farm manager, Jody Alexander, to go check out the mare. (Jody's family had deep roots in the horse business. His uncle was a manager at the well-known Darby Dan Farm in Lexington.) Jody and Kirk came back with a positive report. I then called Paula and said, "I'll buy the mare," which meant we sealed the deal. "Where do I wire the money?" She replied, "Let me find out. I'll get the instructions and call you back in the morning."

The next day, she called me and asked, "Would you take a profit?"

"What do you mean?'" I replied.

She explained that after I bought her, someone looked at the mare, really liked her, and offered $300,000. I said, "Well, Paula, I'm not that smart. I don't know if she's worth $250,000 or $300,000, but I think I'll just keep her. Where do I wire the money?"

She said, "I'll call you back in the morning with the details."

The next morning, she called and asked, "Would you take $350,000 for the mare?" I said, "Paula, something must have happened in the family to make this mare more valuable." She replied, "No, I've checked. They just love her and want to buy her."

I wanted to make sure the buyers would pay Paula's commission, and when they agreed to, I decided to sell. In just forty-eight hours I made $100,000 on a mare I never even saw! That's how crazy the horse industry was in the mid-1980s.

During the spring of 1987, Keeneland ran the Courtland Farm Purse, which meant that our farm paid for the julep cup presented to the owner of the winning horse. A few days after that race I was having lunch at Stoney's and a man named Wayne Lyster approached me to introduce himself. Wayne owns a 350-acre horse farm in Versailles called Ashview, and one of his horses had won the Farm Purse. We struck up an immediate friendship and started attending Keeneland races together. Wayne was a good friend of the politician Brereton Jones, and one day he invited me to his office at Ashview to meet him. During our conversation Brereton said that he was running for lieutenant governor of Kentucky, and he invited me to be his campaign manager, which would involve having me appear at campaign stops to help draw crowds. "I'm going to visit 120 counties over a year," he told me. "And I'd like for you to come with me and to introduce me. Think about this because it's quite a commitment."

That night, I discussed the offer with Cheri and decided to accept. Brereton was afraid I was going to ask for money in return, but I didn't. I said, "When you are elected lieutenant governor, it's almost automatic that you'll be the governor one day. The governor gets to go to the cupola above the winner's circle at the Kentucky Derby. I'll help you, but when you're governor, I want to go to the cupola with you and watch the Derby from the infield."

True to his word, Brereton made campaign stops in every Kentucky county. I'd introduce him, and he'd give his spiel. Early in the campaign we scheduled an event at the Daviess County Fairgrounds in Owensboro, with newspaper, television, and radio ads saying that we'd be giving away twelve autographed basketballs. As we approached the fairgrounds pavilion, Brereton asked our driver, "How many people do you think will be here? A thousand?"

The driver replied, "Oh, no. We don't draw that kind of crowd. There might be a couple hundred."

As we pulled into the parking lot we noticed only about a dozen cars. Once inside the pavilion, the only people assembled were the volunteers and a few fairground staffers. I think everybody in the place got an autographed basketball! If Brereton could have quit his campaign that night he would have, but his campaign really built steam and he won the lieutenant governor election in 1987.

About one month later, before tip-off of a game against Louisville on December 12, the UK Athletic Department raised my number 44 jersey to the rafters of Rupp Arena, which is the ultimate honor for any Wildcat. Cliff Hagan, the athletic director at the time, presented me with a framed UK number 44 jersey. That felt significant because it was Cliff's single-game scoring record that I had broken during my career, a record I held for quite a while until Jodie Meeks eventually surpassed it. (Incidentally, there are three UK players who wore number 44 whose jerseys have been retired at UK: Cotton Nash, Phil Grawemeyer, and me.)

When you think about all the incredible players and legendary teams that have come through Kentucky, and how long the program has stood at the top of college basketball, it's a tremendous honor to be recognized in that way. In my opinion, there are only three true basketball bluebloods:

Prior to Kentucky's game against Louisville on December 12, 1987, my jersey was retired to the rafters at Rupp Arena. I'm pictured with then–athletic director Cliff Hagan. (Courtesy of UK Athletics.)

Kentucky, Kansas, and North Carolina. UCLA has the most championships, of course, but ever since Coach John Wooden retired, that program has been up and down. Indiana was dominant under Coach Knight, but they haven't maintained that level of success. And while Duke was outstanding under Coach K, it wasn't a major program before his arrival. But Kentucky—going all the way back to the 1930s and 1940s—has consistently been one of the premier programs. So, to have my jersey retired at Kentucky, which I truly believe is the best program in the country, is an incredible honor. It's something I'll always be proud of.

Cheri and I experienced about two years of success at Courtland before the bottom dropped out of the market in the late 1980s. By that, I mean that, in addition to the high interest rates and inflation affecting the United States, there was a boom in horse breeding that led to an oversupply of racehorses. As oil prices dropped, so did the value of Thoroughbreds. It was a perfect storm—falling prices and overproduction—that brought the Thoroughbred industry to its knees.

To earn some extra income during that time, I had the opportunity to call several SEC basketball games alongside Tom Hammond, one of the all-time great sports commentators. Tom and I have known each other since my college days. He worked at WLEX-TV in Lexington and called some of our UK games. Over time, we became close friends and even partnered on several horses with our mentor, Tom Gentry. Our families vacationed together, and one of the many values we share is a deep commitment to family.

During the 1987 basketball season, I was invited to provide color analysis for a Vanderbilt game in Nashville, working with another broadcasting legend: Marty Brennaman. Marty is a hero in Kentucky, Ohio, and Indiana because of all the years he spent calling Cincinnati Reds baseball games. I can't remember who the Commodores were playing that night, but it was a thrill to work with someone I had listened to for so many years. What stood out was how kind Marty was to me. On air, he set me up to contribute and helped me find my voice during the broadcast. I was a neophyte, and he was the consummate professional.

In the summer of 1988, Cheri and I decided to sell the farm in order to pay off our debts. Around the same time, I received a phone call from Pete Babcock, the president and general manager of the Nuggets. He offered me a job as assistant general manager for the franchise, along with a role doing color commentary for games alongside Jeff Kingery, the team's radio play-by-play announcer. We decided to move back to Denver, but we left Sheridan behind. It was the start of her junior year in high school, and we didn't want to disrupt her friendships at school and church. She stayed with Cheri's sister, Vicki, and her husband, Gene, for the last two years of school at Woodford County High. It was a difficult situation for us. We missed her, of course, but she came home for the summers and during major school breaks. It was a significant sacrifice for Vicki and Gene, as they never had children of their own, and suddenly they were hosting a high school junior fulltime. They truly stepped up.

As Cheri, Scott, and I settled back in Denver, we looked for a new church home, something as vibrant as the church we had attended in Versailles. Doug Moe's wife, Jane, suggested that we try Cherry Creek Presbyterian, a church founded by Pastor Mark Brewer. One Sunday, we got ready and headed over. As we were just a few blocks from the church, traffic suddenly became stop-and-go. One of my biggest pet peeves (or maybe just a sign of my impatience) is waiting in line. I hate it. I said, "This is ridiculous. I don't want to do this."

But Cheri insisted. She said, "No, Jane told me this would happen. She said to go over to the high school and park; there are shuttle buses."

Well, the shuttle bus turned out to be a yellow school bus. I didn't even fit in the seat properly. I was perched on the edge, knees sticking out into the aisle. When we finally got to the church, it was packed. We ended up sitting on two folding chairs along the back wall.

But within five minutes of being there, I knew that this was where we belonged. Two things stood out to me that day. First, the music. It was phenomenal. And second, Brewer's message. He presents the Word of God in a way that feels relevant to your everyday life and what you're going through. That combination—truth, humor, and real-life application—is what really resonated with me. Cherry Creek Presbyterian soon became our home church.

Not long after that, we invited Mark and Carolyn to dinner at one of our favorite restaurants. Mark arrived right on time and told us, "Carolyn's right behind me." We figured they were coming in two cars, but twenty, maybe twenty-five minutes went by before Carolyn showed up.

We found out later that in her rush she had grabbed a pair of white shoes out of the closet. One was a high heel, and the other was a flat. She had gotten in the car barefoot and didn't realize the mismatch until they were nearly at the restaurant, so she dropped Mark off and made a detour to a shoe store to buy a matching pair before joining us! That dinner marked the beginning of a wonderful friendship. Over the years, Mark and Carolyn have been by our side through so many seasons of life.

While our personal lives were being enriched by these new friendships, my professional life was going through some changes as well. Since Doug Moe was still the Nuggets' head coach, I was already familiar with the style of play I would be commenting on during broadcasts. However, after the 1989–1990 season, the Nuggets parted ways with Pete Babcock and hired Kentucky native Bernie Bickerstaff as their general manager. Bernie replaced Doug Moe with Paul Westhead, a former Loyola Marymount University coach known for his up-tempo style of play. This transition also marked the end of my role as assistant general manager. For the following two seasons, I continued working as a color analyst alongside the legendary play-by-play announcer Eddie Doucette.

During that stretch, the Nuggets had one of the worst records in the NBA, so it posed a challenge to be a color commentator for the team and have nice things to say. Paul Westhead's offensive strategy during his days coaching Loyola Marymount was to have players shoot within the first eight seconds of having the ball on their side of the court. He tried to replicate that style in the NBA and the scores were astronomical. One time we were in Phoenix playing the Suns, and the Suns scored more than one hundred points in the first half! The end of those seasons did not come soon enough. However, an unexpected opportunity arose that would allow me to step away from my broadcast career.

In December of 1991, Brereton Jones was sworn in as governor of Kentucky, and in early 1992 he called to offer me a job as secretary of tourism, knowing I couldn't begin until my commitment as a color analyst with the Nuggets ended after the 1991–92 season. I even traveled to Frankfort and saw the office I would have if I accepted the offer. But something unexpected happened. While I was in Sacramento preparing for one of the last road games of the 1991–92 Nuggets season, Bickerstaff called me. Apparently, he liked what I was saying on the television broadcasts and asked, "Have you ever thought about coaching?"

"Coaching who?" I asked.

"Coaching the Denver Nuggets."

"No."

"Well, when you get home tomorrow, I want you to come to my office and we'll talk about it."

Meanwhile, we had rented a house in Versailles, and Cheri had the mother of all garage sales because we were in the process of moving back to Kentucky, thinking I'd accept the secretary of tourism job. Word got out somehow on a local radio station that the Issels were having a garage sale. Unbeknownst to me, Cheri had put some of my clothes in it. So many people showed up that a local policeman came by to direct traffic.

After returning from Sacramento, I said to her, "We need to talk over lunch." She and I went to our favorite Greek restaurant. When the server came by to ask what we wanted to drink, I said, "She'll have a glass of wine, and I'll have a beer." Cheri responded, "I'm not having a glass of wine for lunch."

I said, "Believe me, you need a glass of wine."

I then told her I had a meeting later that afternoon with Bernie to discuss the possibility of coaching the Nuggets. She was surprised, especially since I had never coached basketball at any level. I've made a lot of smart decisions in my life, but I've also done my fair share of stupid things. Through it all, Cheri has always supported me, which is why we've had such a strong marriage. After she expressed her concern about my lack of coaching experience, I reassured her that I believed I could do it. She knew this was something I was passionate about, and once she understood that, she was fully on board.

A few hours after our lunch I met with Bernie to explore the possibility of becoming head coach. The process took several weeks, as other candidates were also being considered. Just a few days after the garage sale, Cheri and I attended the Nuggets' last game of the season. We were seated in the arena when a rather large man walked up to me and said, "How do you like my sport coat?" I looked at it and replied, "That's *my* sport coat." That's when Cheri finally confessed—she'd sold some of my clothes at the garage sale.

In the meantime, our family moved out of the house we'd been renting and back into the two-bedroom suite at the nearby Sheraton hotel! I also called Brereton to inform him there was a possibility that I might become the head coach of the Nuggets. I asked if he could hold the position a little longer, as they had already announced it. Previously, I had been interviewed by Barbara Bailey, a WKYT newscaster in Lexington and good friend of ours, over the phone about the secretary of tourism position, so it was already out there.

One night, as negotiations with Bernie about the Nuggets job continued, Cheri and I were in bed watching the ten o'clock news when Ron Zappolo, a dear friend of ours who had been a sportscaster in Denver for years, came on. He said, "A source just called and said they saw Don Chaney at the Denver airport, and he will be the next coach of the Denver Nuggets." Don had been a shooting guard for the Celtics and a coach for the Houston Rockets.

Cheri turned to me, shocked, and said, "What's going on? What is he talking about? Why has Bernie kept us in Denver and not told us he was going to hire someone else to be the coach?"

I said, "Honey, all I can tell you is that Bernie's been talking to me."

It turned out that the person spotted at the airport was not Don Chaney, but rather someone who looked like him.

Meanwhile, during one of my next conversations with Bernie, he asked who I would want as my assistant coaches if I were to land the job. My top choice was Gene Littles. Gene had been a teammate of mine on the Colonels, and we even shared a locker during our championship season. He later went on to coach the Cleveland Cavaliers and the Charlotte Hornets.

I knew he was also one of the candidates Bernie was considering for the head coach position, which I think helped solidify my chances. After our conversation, Bernie flew Gene in to gauge his interest in becoming my assistant coach, should I be offered the head coach role. Gene was all in, and about a week later Bernie offered me the job in person. He really took a chance on me. I had never coached at any level, not even junior high, but he hired me as the head coach of the Nuggets!

I called Brereton to thank him for the offer to join his cabinet as secretary of tourism, but I let him know that I had accepted the head coach position with the team. "You can't turn that down," he said. My starting salary was $800,000 per year, slightly higher than what I had made during my last season playing for the Nuggets. A new chapter, a new challenge. I couldn't help but feel that this was exactly where I was meant to be.

9

From Court to Clipboard

My first season coaching the Nuggets was one of the true blessings of my life. It was so much fun, with Gene Littles as my first assistant coach and my former Nuggets teammate Mike Evans as my second assistant coach. Our core unit included Dikembe Mutombo from Georgetown, Mahmoud Abdul-Rauf (who was known as Chris Jackson during his days playing at LSU), and two rookies: LaPhonso Ellis from Notre Dame and Bryant Stith from Virginia. These guys worked their tails off.

Since this was my first coaching experience, I tried to incorporate the best qualities of my previous coaches to develop my own style. I didn't want to be a taskmaster, especially because the team had endured two tough losing seasons and didn't need someone imposing authority over them. They needed positivity, someone who was more of a mentor than a traditional coach. That's what I aimed to be.

From Coach Rupp, I adopted his belief that winning was everything. Individual accolades weren't the focus; winning the game was. I emphasized to the team that whatever they wanted from the game—whether it was a long-term contract, endorsements, or financial security—came through winning, not the other way around. Fortunately, we had great players who were eager to turn things around, as they all came from successful college programs. They committed themselves to putting in the work.

Hubie Brown was the best-prepared coach I ever played for. From him, I learned the importance of being ready for each game—doing the film work, studying, and preparing for our opponents.

Larry Brown was the best teacher I ever played for. He was one of the few coaches to find success in both college and professional basketball. He won an NBA championship with Detroit and a national championship with the Kansas Jayhawks. From him, I learned the importance of individual coaching—not just focusing on the team as a whole, but on developing each player individually.

Doug Moe, on the other hand, was more complex. When the game wasn't in progress, Doug was laid-back, didn't do much preparation, and wasn't overly concerned with the strategy of our opponents. He focused more on his own approach. But once the game started, he transformed into a completely different person: wild, intense, and full of energy, often yelling and swearing. From him, I took the positive aspects—his laid-back approach, not being too hard on myself, and carrying that mindset into the game.

The most difficult adjustment for me early on was leading pregame talks and, especially, diagramming plays on the whiteboard. I'd seen it and heard it thousands of times, but I had never actually done it myself. That was the biggest challenge in transitioning to a head coach in the NBA.

I vividly remember my first regular-season game as a coach. We hosted the San Antonio Spurs, and I wore a brown suit in honor of Coach Rupp. The Spurs were coached by Jerry Tarkanian, who was new to the NBA but didn't last long. His success with the UNLV Runnin' Rebels didn't translate to the pro level. Sometimes that happens. Anyway, Dikembe fouled out, so from there on LaPhonso, who was playing in his very first NBA game, had the tough task of guarding David Robinson, who was a force. We won the game in double overtime, 125–121, but I didn't have time to celebrate with Cheri, my kids, or my friends because after the game we boarded a plane and flew to Portland for our next match. The Trail Blazers beat us soundly, 123–104. It was a quick lesson that the excitement of winning is often short-lived, while losing brings you back to reality.

Around this time, I had a shift in my spiritual life when Mark Brewer left Cherry Creek Presbyterian to become the lead pastor at Ward Presbyterian Church in Township, Michigan, a Detroit suburb. During a trip to Detroit, when I was coaching a game against the Pistons, Mark came

Cheri and I visiting our dear friends Mark and Carolyn Brewer, 2025.

to the game with three of his elders. Afterward, as we were talking, he asked, "Do you mind if I ride back on the bus with you to the hotel?"

Mark shared that while he was doing well, Carolyn and the kids were struggling in Detroit, and he was hoping to return to Denver. When Mark returned in 1993, he came without a church to pastor. However, Cheri and I, along with two other couples from Cherry Creek Presbyterian, pledged to guarantee his salary for six months. This support enabled him to start Colorado Community Church in Englewood. Being part of that church's development was one of the most rewarding experiences I've ever had. I served on the board, and it was very rewarding to see all the new people who were coming to know Christ. The church grew quickly, and within a year we were able to purchase an existing church building. Cheri and I made many new friends there, and we were co-chairs of the new building campaign.

In 1998, Cheri and I joined the church board members and their spouses on a trip to Israel, led by Mark and Carolyn Brewer. We were there for a little over a week and visited all the major sites, including Bethlehem, the Wailing Wall, and the Garden of Gethsemane. But for me, the most unforgettable moment came when Mark baptized the entire church board in the Jordan River. We had all brought our bathing suits, knowing it might happen, but nothing could have prepared me for how powerful that experience would be. It's a memory I'll carry with me for the rest of my life.

Back in the basketball world, the Nuggets finished the 1992–93 season with a 36–46 record but still missed the playoffs. Nevertheless, I felt we were on the brink of turning the program around. After the season ended, Cheri, Sheridan, and I attended the 119th running of the Kentucky Derby on May 1, 1993. By then, Brereton had become the governor of Kentucky, and he invited us to join his entourage on a special train ride from Frankfort to Louisville on race day. Once we arrived at Churchill Downs, we settled into a clubhouse room on the sixth floor. We were seated at a table when, about forty-five minutes before the Derby, a state trooper tapped me on the shoulder and asked Cheri and me to follow him. We left Sheridan behind.

The trooper led us down a back stairwell that took us to an entrance to the track. He escorted us across the track and up to the cupola above the winner's circle. It hit me that Brereton was fulfilling the request I made when he asked for my help with his lieutenant governor campaign, even though we hadn't discussed it since. Once we reached the cupola, Brereton and his wife, Libby, were there waiting for us, along with Tom Meeker, the president of Churchill Downs, and his wife, Carol. From that perch, we watched jockey Jerry Bailey ride Sea Hero to victory in the Kentucky Derby. That was a "wow" moment for us.

Just nine days later, another unforgettable experience followed: I was inducted into the Naismith Memorial Basketball Hall of Fame, in Springfield, Massachusetts. Back in February, I'd received a call notifying me that I had been elected to the Class of 1993. Though honored, I was stunned. The enshrinement ceremony and related events, which took place on May 10, turned out to be incredible. My entire family attended: Cheri, Sheridan, Scott, my parents, my siblings, and Cheri's parents; and we had a great time.

Each inductee was given five minutes to speak. My fellow inductees were Walt Bellamy, Julius Erving, Dick McGuire, Ann Meyers, Calvin Murphy, Soviet Olympic standout Uljana Semjonova, and Bill Walton.

Dick McGuire, who was terrified of public speaking, gave a very brief speech. He got up and said, "Thank you very much. I want to thank my wife and my family," and sat down. That was about it. The rest of us stuck pretty closely to the five-minute limit.

My speech involved a string of thank-yous, including to my former coaches, teammates, friends, extended family, and to Cheri and my children. "When I talk about my career, I use the term 'we' quite a bit," I said. "It really has been a partnership. Cheri has done the important things, like raise the family and run the household while I was out pursuing my dream of being a basketball player."

Then Walton—who, because of the alphabetical order, went last—decided to critique everyone's career who had just been inducted. He must have talked for about twenty-five minutes. We were all just shaking our heads, thinking, "That's Bill."

One funny story I remember from that weekend involved my good friend Denny McGowan—the former assistant general manager with the Nuggets—and his wife, Gayle. They attended the ceremony and hosted a little party in their hotel room. They even set up a full bar. My Uncle Floyd and Aunt Phyllis were there, too. We stayed up pretty late that night, enjoying ourselves in Denny's room. Then, at eight o'clock the next morning, there was a knock at Denny's hotel door. He and Gayle were still sleeping. Denny opened the door, and there was my Uncle Floyd.

He said, "Is the bar open yet?" At 8 a.m.!

During the 1993–94 season, the Nuggets compiled a 42–40 record and qualified for the playoffs as an eighth seed. In the first round we faced the number one seed, the Seattle SuperSonics, who had Shawn Kemp and Gary Payton. We lost the first two games in Seattle—both by double digits—but we won games 3 and 4 in Denver to tie the series. That really put the pressure on Seattle, because no eighth seed had ever won an NBA playoff series against a one seed. By this time the Nuggets were taking chartered flights on 727 and 737 aircraft to away games, and there were always empty seats on the plane. Guys would often ask me, "Can I bring my brother on the trip?" or, "Can I bring my cousin?" As we prepared to head for the decisive game five, Dikembe and LaPhonso walked into my office and said, "Coach, we think we should bring someone special on the trip."

"Who do you have in mind?" I asked.

"Bo Mitchell," they replied.

Bo had played both basketball and baseball at the University of Colorado Boulder. He was instrumental in starting several churches in Denver and eventually became our chaplain. At that time, every NBA team had a chaplain who would lead a ten- to fifteen-minute service before the game, not only for the home team but also for any visiting players who wished to attend. A handful of Nuggets players, including Dikembe and LaPhonso, regularly participated in Bo's chapel service.

Bo traveled with us to Seattle, where his pregame message, drawing inspiration from the story of David versus Goliath, boosted the players' confidence and helped them believe they could win. I remember adding, "Don't worry about playing great. Just play as hard as you can and we'll live with the results." We were clear underdogs when the game tipped off on May 7, 1994, but against the odds, we defeated Seattle in overtime, 98–94. That victory made us the first eighth-seed team to ever defeat a top-seed team in NBA playoff history.

"No bookie, no bettor, no armchair quarterback, no 76-year-old grandmother sipping Metamucil in a nursing home could have thought this would happen," Nuggets forward Brian Williams was quoted as saying after the win.[1] He scored seventeen points and pulled down nineteen rebounds in the game, while Robert Pack led our team in scoring with twenty-three points. Dikembe blocked eight shots. Winning that series was the highlight of my coaching career.

In the second round of the playoffs we faced the Utah Jazz, who had John Stockton, Karl Malone, and Jeff Hornacek. We found ourselves down 3–0 in the series, which was a best-of-seven. Despite the tough start, we won game four in Denver and then headed back to Salt Lake City for game five. We hadn't won a game there in ages, but we managed to pull off a victory. We won game six at home, but the Jazz beat us in game seven on their home court, 91–81, and that marked the end of our playoff run.

During the start of the 1994–95 season, things started to fall apart. In the preseason, LaPhonso suffered a stress fracture of his right kneecap in a pickup game with Bryant Stith, a knee injury that sidelined him for most of the season. It's interesting how the culture of a team can be so important, especially in the locker room. Not only did we lose LaPhonso, but Bryant Stith missed some games with an ankle injury. Then there was Mahmoud Abdul-Rauf, who had converted to Islam. As a Christian, I don't share the same beliefs as Mahmoud, but I was always impressed by how devoted he became to his faith. However, it wasn't his religion that affected him—it was his lifestyle. He wasn't resting properly, wasn't eating right, and his performance on the court took a hit. There was also some jealousy in the locker room over endorsements and things like that, which added to the tension.

By the middle of the season we were hovering around .500. One day, Charlie Lyons, who was president and CEO of both the Nuggets and the Colorado Avalanche at the time, called me. He told me to go to Bernie's office forty-five minutes before our game; Bernie wanted to talk. I thought he was going to offer advice or encouragement, but when I walked into Bernie's office I saw a calculator on his desk. He was working out my contract buyout.

"Bernie, if you're getting ready to fire me, I'm not taking a penny less than what you owe me," I told him. I still had another year left on my contract, and I wasn't willing to leave without getting everything I was owed.

We had a good, cordial conversation, and in the end we decided it was time for me to step aside. But I still coached that night. To my knowledge, nobody but Bernie and Charlie Lyons knew it was going to be my last game. Afterward, I met with Cheri and told her what had happened. She seemed more relieved than anything else, as the job had become all-consuming. Then I met with the assistant coaches.

"Who's going to coach the team?" Gene Littles asked.

"I think you are, Gene," I said.

Gene wasn't keen on the idea, but he eventually agreed to take over as head coach halfway through that season.

It was the first time I had ever been fired. There was some consolation knowing I had a year and a half of salary left. I thought that, because of the success I'd had, I might get another coaching opportunity elsewhere. But that didn't happen. Maybe I didn't do as good of a job as I thought, or maybe it was because of my ties to the Nuggets organization. Regardless, I found myself at a crossroads, which led me to a new chapter in Denver.

I had befriended a local attorney, Doug Sykes, who shared my passion for Thoroughbreds. Doug eventually decided he no longer wanted to practice law and had a client who owned a printing business called Keogh and Company. The client was looking to retire, so Doug and I bought the company. I began working there full-time, from nine to five. One of our clients was Coors beer in Golden, Colorado. They had a catalog for their distributors that included a variety of promotional items, like pens and pencils—a thick book with all sorts of things in it. We also produced large three-by-ten-foot banners for the company, as well as point-of-sale items for other clients. It was fulfilling work, and we were doing well financially.

While Doug and I were building momentum with the printing business, another opportunity came my way. In 1997, I had the pleasure of calling a few NBA games for NBC Sports alongside Tom Hammond. I'll never forget the time we were in New York covering a Knicks game. Our good friends Bill and Barbara Goldy were with us. Cheri had already seen her fair share of basketball games, so they decided to skip the Knicks game. Instead, they opted for a matinee of a Broadway play. On their way to the theater, though, they walked past the Times Square Jumbotron—and there we were! Tom and I were live, doing our pregame show on the massive screen. Cheri couldn't escape me.

I had been out of the leadership loop of the NBA for a while, but the buzz among Denver sports fans was about how badly the 1997–98 Nuggets were struggling. They won only eleven games that year, which still stands as the worst record in franchise history. In January of 1998, Charlie Lyons called me up and invited me to meet with Nuggets general manager Allan Bristow to discuss a potential position within the organization. I agreed and met with Bristow for about ten minutes. He didn't mention anything about me joining the Nuggets but instead encouraged me to run for mayor of Denver. "We'll give you all the support you need," he said.

"Allan, I have no interest in being the mayor of Denver," I replied, and I got up and left.

A few weeks later, my dad and I were at a sports bar in Denver while Cheri and my mom were shopping nearby. Charlie walked in to pick up a to-go order. I was less than friendly, giving him the cold shoulder—didn't even introduce him to my dad or anything—and he left. The next day, Charlie called me and asked, "Are you mad at me?"

I told him, "No, Charlie, I'm not mad at you. But you mentioned talking to Allan Bristow about me joining the organization, but Allan told me he wanted me to run for mayor of Denver."

Charlie was stunned. "You're kidding me?" he asked.

"No, that's exactly what happened," I replied.

During the All-Star break, with the Nuggets holding a 4–42 record, Charlie fired Bristow and hired me as the general manager of the Denver Nuggets. I was excited about the opportunity to help turn things around. However, about a week into the job, on February 12, 1998, to be exact, I received the devastating news that my brother, Greg, had passed away from a heart attack. He was only forty-six. Even though he lived nineteen years after his kidney transplant, his loss was still overwhelming for all of us, especially my parents.

After my dad retired, Greg took over Issel Painting and Decorating, the Batavia business my dad had started, and grew it significantly. He achieved great success. But his sudden passing was a shock to everyone. We knew Greg had struggled with high blood pressure, but you never expect someone to die of a heart attack at such a young age.

Greg and I were always in touch by phone. He loved the Thoroughbred industry as much as I did, and we both followed sports. We'd also see each other in the summertime. During the NBA season, he would attend all the games we played in Chicago. He was my best friend growing up, and I truly miss him. But as with every tragedy in my life, my faith is what helped me get through. Greg, too, was a man of faith. Given the many physical challenges he endured, it brings some comfort knowing that we can be sure of where he is now. Greg is buried in the same Batavia cemetery as my parents and grandparents.

I continued to process the loss of Greg as I began my role as general manager, which involved making some difficult decisions. By the end of the season, I had to fire Coach Bill Hanzlik and his assistant, T. R. Dunn, both of whom were friends and former Nuggets teammates of mine. We decided to hire another assistant, Mike D'Antoni, as the new head coach. He brought in John Lucas as his top assistant. The Nuggets held the third pick in that year's NBA draft, so we were involved in the selection process.

In the midst of these significant decisions with the team, life outside of basketball brought its own important moments. On June 20, 1998, four days before the NBA draft, our family gathered in Denver to celebrate the wedding of our daughter, Sheridan, to Rick Whipple, a native of San Juan Capistrano. Sheridan and Rick met while attending Northwestern University, but they didn't start dating until after college, when they both landed jobs in Chicago. Rick was an exceptional high school baseball pitcher and earned a full scholarship to play at Northwestern. His impressive performance continued there until, as often happens with pitchers, he injured both his shoulder and elbow. That marked the end of his baseball career.

When Rick and Sheridan decided to get married, Rick came to me to ask for my permission, which I thought was a thoughtful, old-fashioned gesture. Cheri and I gave Sheridan an unlimited budget for the wedding, and, of course, she ended up exceeding it. The ceremony took place at

The Issel family at Sheridan and Rick's wedding, held at Colorado Community Church on June 20, 1998. The ceremony was officiated by Mark Brewer.

Colorado Community Church, with Mark Brewer officiating. The most special moment for me was walking Sheridan down the aisle. We held the reception at the Denver Petroleum Club, located in a high-rise building in downtown Denver.

Meanwhile, back in the basketball world, our focus shifted to the NBA draft. The player we really liked was Paul Pierce, who played for Roy Williams at Kansas. But we needed a big guy, and Kansas also had Raef LaFrentz. I called Williams, who gave me a glowing report on Raef: "Great family, great kid," he said. "Raef plays the game like you did. He can run the floor and has a nice outside jump shot."

I then asked him about Paul Pierce.

"Paul hangs around with some bad people," Williams told me. "I wouldn't touch Paul Pierce with a ten-foot pole."

Apparently, Roy was saying the same thing to other general managers, which caused Pierce to fall to the tenth spot in the first round, where the Celtics selected him. There, Pierce went on to have a Hall of Fame career.

In March of 2025, I attended an autograph event for former pro athletes in Chicago, and Paul was there. He approached me and gave me a hug. I said, "Paul, the biggest regret I have is not drafting you."

He replied, "Hey, it all worked out."

I said, "It worked out for you, but not for me!"

The Nuggets faced a difficult 1998–99 season due to the NBA lockout between team owners and players over salary caps and salaries, which led to the season being reduced to just fifty games. We finished with a record of 14–36. During that brief season, it became clear that Mike D'Antoni had lost the locker room to John Lucas. For instance, there were times when D'Antoni would stand on the sideline and call a play, only for Lucas to stand up behind him and call a different play. The team would then run the play that Lucas called. Eventually, D'Antoni was calling for Lucas to be fired. He also wanted to trade away some of our key players, such as Nick Van Exel, which created tension.

As a result of the lockout, the Nuggets' owners, Communications Satellite Corporation (Comsat), decided to sell the team. As a publicly traded company, Comsat realized that owning a sports franchise wasn't the best fit for their business. Bill Laurie, a Missouri-based businessman and philanthropist and the son-in-law of the late James "Bud" Walton, cofounder of Walmart, proposed purchasing the Nuggets and the Avalanche for around $425 to $450 million. Charlie Lyons proposed taking a 10 percent stake in the deal. Under the plan, Bill Laurie would own 90 percent while Charlie Lyons would hold the rest.

On May 1, 1999, I was hosting a Kentucky Derby watch party for about thirty people when Charlie called. "I want you to come to lunch with me and Bill Laurie," he insisted. I left my own Derby party to meet them.

Over lunch, Bill Laurie told me he was going to buy the team, that everything was set, but he wanted me to fire D'Antoni and return to the bench as head coach. The idea of firing Mike wasn't something I took lightly. I didn't have a strong desire to return to coaching, knowing how it would affect me. In the meantime, Dean Bonham, a former president of the Nuggets, had started his own sports consulting group in Denver and was asked by local media to estimate the team's value. He put the price between $500 million and $550 million. When the board at Comsat saw this, they believed Charlie was making a sweetheart deal, selling the team for a lowball offer from Bill Laurie. In response, Comsat hired lawyers, and both Bill and Charlie were quickly removed from the running as potential owners of the Nuggets. Although Comsat still owned the team, there was no CEO or president in place. I was left to manage the Nuggets organization on my own, with D'Antoni still serving as coach, while Pierre Lacroix, the general manager of the Avalanche, was handling that franchise alone as well. It was complete chaos.

The next person to enter the picture was Colorado businessman and philanthropist Donald Sturm, who outbid a group of investors that included former Denver Broncos quarterback John Elway. On July 26, 1999, he offered $461 million to acquire the Nuggets, the Avalanche, and the Pepsi Center, which was set to open on October 1 of that year.[2] Sturm believed he was getting a great deal, especially since the seller claimed the value was between $500 million and $550 million.

He was a kind man, though I'm not sure he fully understood what he was getting into. He never went anywhere without his wife and his accountant. We had a meeting in his office, located in Cherry Creek—less than five miles from McNichols Arena, where the teams were still playing before the Pepsi Center opened. As we were preparing to leave for McNichols, where Sturm was scheduled to address the employees about purchasing the two teams, he asked, "Can I follow you? I'm not sure how to get to McNichols Arena."

Sturm was doing his due diligence, but during a meeting with Pierre Lacroix, me, and his accountant, one thing that really bothered him was that employees were given two season tickets. He also mentioned that the employee parking lot was one of the prime lots at the Pepsi Center. "On game nights, I want the employees to park in the back parking lot," he told us. He continued, "And instead of each employee getting two season tickets, we'll create a pool of tickets. Employees can make requests, and once the pool runs out, that's it."

He added, "I understand the Nashville Predators do this." Then, with a straight face, he looked at Pierre and me and asked, "Are they hockey or basketball?"

In a separate, private conversation with Sturm about the Nuggets, we discussed the issues with D'Antoni—particularly his friction with Lucas and his desire to trade away key players. I brought up my previous conversation with Laurie, where he suggested parting ways with D'Antoni and having me take over as coach. Sturm agreed that this was the right move. So, in September of 1999, before Sturm's official purchase of the franchise was finalized, I fired Mike and named myself as the head coach.

Starting my second run as Nuggets head coach in our brand-new locker room at the Pepsi Center.

I'm sure many people thought, "Issel's got a huge ego; he just wants to go back to coaching." But the truth is, I had no intention of going back to the bench. I knew what it was like, and I knew how it affected me. But my decision to fire Mike was premature. About six months later, Sturm's acquisition deal fell through when he refused to guarantee that the team would remain in Denver for twenty-five years.

Coaching the team during the ownership turmoil was a miserable experience. However, on July 6, 2000, billionaire businessman Stan Kroenke stepped in to purchase the Nuggets, the Avalanche, and the Pepsi Center (now Ball Arena) for $450 million.[3] The deal included a clause that committed the Nuggets to Denver for the next twenty-five years. Everyone was relieved to finally have some stability, and as of this writing Stan remains the team's owner. (Interestingly, his wife, Ann, is Bud Walton's other daughter.)

Stan was very focused on the basketball side of things. He allowed Pierre to handle decisions regarding the Avalanche but was deeply involved in basketball-related decisions. One thing I remember about him is that in almost every meeting he would pull out a large stack of checks from his briefcase and sign them while we talked. I once asked him, "Don't you have a CFO or someone who could handle all these checks?"

"This is how I stay on top of my companies," he replied. "I sign every check and review every invoice, from the biggest to the smallest."

I found that fascinating. It really demonstrated how hands-on he was. Of course, with the number of businesses and sports teams he owns now, it would likely be impossible for him to manage that way. But at the time it was an impressive approach.

10

Lost Joy

When Stan took over as owner of the Nuggets, he became heavily involved in basketball matters, and it quickly became clear that he intended to bring in his own people. One of the first things Stan did was ask, "Who's this military guy calling around the league talking about trades?"

He was referring to our assistant general manager, Denny McGowan, who was a Big Brother from my fraternity days at UK. Denny had dropped out of college, joined the army, and served two tours in Vietnam—first as an infantryman and then as a helicopter pilot. Both were among the most dangerous roles in the military. A career military man, Denny had transitioned to civilian life in Denver, where I hired him as my assistant general manager. His attention to detail was invaluable to me, especially since, honestly, I wasn't great at negotiating contracts. I needed someone tougher than me to handle that.

When I explained to Stan who Denny was, he replied, "Well, we don't need him." So, one of the first things I had to do was fire Denny, which ultimately strained a lifelong friendship. Stan also hired my old teammate, Kiki VanDeWeghe, as president of the organization, which diminished some of the power I had.

This shift in leadership had a significant impact on team chemistry and my ability to secure the caliber of players we needed. Personally, it was a tough time. We had a veteran team, some of whom were nearing the end of their careers, and I made several poor decisions along the way.

For example, I selected Raef LaFrentz over Paul Pierce and Vince Carter in the 1998 NBA draft—a decision I regret in hindsight. I also made a questionable trade, acquiring Ron Mercer from the Celtics in exchange for Bryant Stith and Chris Herren—two of my favorite players. At the time, Ron seemed like a great addition, but there was more to the story. Rick Pitino, the Celtics' coach at the time, had told Mercer that he was being traded because the team couldn't offer him a long-term contract, and that Denver would be willing to do so. So, Ron showed up with his agent, expecting a long-term deal in the final year of his Celtics contract.

I'll never forget sitting in a suite at a downtown hotel with Ron, his agent, and Denny (before I had to let him go). Ron's agent confidently said, "We think Ron is the next Michael Jordan." I had to bite my tongue to keep from laughing. I wanted to ask how many times Michael Jordan had been traded, but I knew that could sour the conversation.

When Ron realized we weren't offering him a long-term contract, his attitude seemed to wane. It was a difficult period for me and my assistant coaches. Our record wasn't great, and the team's effort fluctuated depending on their perception of the game. When they thought we had a chance to win, they played hard. But when we faced stronger opponents, the enthusiasm wasn't there.

In December of 2000, we were coming off a winless four-game road trip. The final game was in Boston, where the Celtics won in overtime on a last-second shot by Paul Pierce. I was incredibly frustrated. After the game, we boarded a flight back to Denver. The headwinds were so strong that we had to land in Minneapolis to refuel. We didn't get home until around three in the morning. And then—like an idiot—I scheduled a practice for later that same day, after a week-long road trip and an overnight flight.

What I still don't understand is that none of my assistant coaches told me how bad of an idea it was. There I was, sitting alone in the practice facility, and no one showed up. Eventually, Mike Evans, one of my assistants, came in. I asked, "Where is everybody?" And he said, "They're not coming."

I said, "What do you mean they're not coming?"

"They're boycotting the practice," he said. "They don't think it's fair."

And honestly, the players were right. You don't call practice as a punishment. That's not how you lead. I was mad and bullheaded, and it's something I should never have done. We practiced the following day and moved on to the next game, but I don't think my relationship with the players was ever the same after that.

The joy of winning started to feel hollow, always overshadowed by the dread of losing. I became a different person, obsessed with figuring out what I could do differently to be a successful coach. I felt constant pressure to change the situation, wondering how I could make things better. As a result, I wasn't as good of a husband or father. It was a miserable period of my life, and I eventually snapped.

On December 11, 2001, the Nuggets hosted the Charlotte Hornets. The game went down to the wire, and one of our veteran players, George McCloud, missed a layup at the end of the game, and we lost—our fifth defeat in a row. Frustrated beyond words, I was heading into the tunnel toward the locker room when a fan began mercilessly taunting me from the stands. I looked up and saw that he appeared to be Hispanic. I yelled, "Go drink another beer, you Mexican piece of shit!" and kept on walking.

A news camera captured the incident, and it was broadcast for the world to see. I was incredibly embarrassed and regret that it became part of my legacy with the Nuggets. Some people may have assumed that, because I played on an all-white team at Kentucky, there was a racial aspect to my remarks. That was never the case for me. I was raised in Northern Illinois and grew up with African American teammates and friends. I've always hoped that I never saw people in terms of black, white, or brown.

The next day, NBA Commissioner David Stern suspended me for four games without pay, and the Nuggets held a press conference attended by members of the Hispanic media and local Hispanic community. Some members of the Hispanic Chamber of Commerce demanded that I be fired.

"I apologize to the fans, to the Nuggets organization and the people of Denver for that uncaring and un-Christian-type comment," I said that day.[1] "I take full responsibility for my actions, and I'm sorry for the embarrassment it's caused my team, my family." I also met privately with leaders of two Hispanic groups in Denver to offer my apologies. Additionally, I apologized to Cheri, my kids, and my parents. A couple of weeks later, I made the decision to resign and accepted a buyout offer.

"Head coaching in this league is a lot of pressure," VanDeWeghe said at a December 27 press conference announcing my decision.[2] "I think December 11 might have just been the result of some of the pressures. We had gone through a rough stretch where we had lost a few in a row,

I made a public apology to members of the Hispanic community as Colorado State Senator Rob Hernandez, D-Denver *(left)*, and State Representative Frana Mace, D-Denver (*right*), look on during a news conference in Denver on December 19, 2001. (AP Images, photograph by David Zalubowski.)

and that builds up. His decision, I don't think, had a lot to do with that incident. I think it was more of an overall thing. I did sense that Dan was troubled by some things and, at times, a little frustrated. Dan, being the competitor he is, when he's not winning, he's frustrated."

Looking back, I don't know why the camera was there in that arena tunnel, but maybe it was God rescuing me from the situation. Once I was out of the picture as head coach, I felt relieved—not having to go down to the Pepsi Center and deal with it anymore.

One thing I remember is Charles Barkley coming to my defense during a television broadcast. He said that instead of yelling back at the fan, I should have gone up into the stands and fought him. I'll never forget that. That was Charles's take on the incident.

It took me years to move past the embarrassment of my comment. I beat myself up about it and became somewhat of a recluse. I'd be out in public, or at the Denver airport, where people would recognize me, and I'd wonder what they were thinking about me. But most people who approached me expressed words of support. It was almost like they forgave me before I forgave myself. Cheri helped me the most during that time. She'd tell me things like, "You've got to let this go. You've prayed for forgiveness, and people have forgiven you. So, you have to forgive yourself."

Eventually, the old Dan reappeared.

Following my resignation from the Nuggets, Cheri and I moved to Singletree, a neighborhood in Edwards, Colorado, just west of Vail. We had owned one half of a duplex there since the 1990s, while our friends, the Goldys, owned the other half. After Scott earned his bachelor's degree from the University of Colorado in 2001, he moved in with us, and we quickly realized we needed more space. So, we sold our half of the duplex and bought a larger, single-family home in the same development.

It turned out that the man who built our duplex also owned the Tile Warehouse in Edwards and was planning to move to Scottsdale, Arizona, to continue his homebuilding business. In July 2002, I partnered with Scott to purchase and run the Tile Warehouse. Builders and designers would come in to select tiles, and we offered a wide range of products—floor tiles, bathroom tiles, backsplashes, kitchen tiles, and more, including some beautiful decorative pieces. We also sold all the supplies needed to lay the tiles, making it a solid business.

During this time, we established a tradition with the Goldys. Nearly every weeknight the four of us gathered to watch *Wheel of Fortune* and play along together. One night, I realized that *Wheel of Fortune* aired an hour earlier in Arkansas, where my mom and dad lived. So, I called my mom and said, "I want you to write down every puzzle from the show tonight and then call me with the answers."

That night, as we played along, I let the first puzzle get about halfway revealed before I "guessed" it. As the show went on, I started solving the puzzles with fewer and fewer letters showing. I was on a roll and no one suspected a thing. After the show ended, I came clean. I admitted I'd called my mom and gotten all the answers ahead of time. Totally cheated!

Around then, I also became a cowboy. Our veterinarian from Lexington, Kirk Shiner, had moved back to his native state of Colorado and had a ranch not far from Edwards. I bought a horse and some cattle to run alongside his herd. Occasionally, I'd put on my cowboy hat, chaps, and boots and join in on cattle drives, moving the cows from one location to another. Growing up on a farm and having a deep love for agriculture, this was something I truly enjoyed.

Another highlight of that year was the arrival of our first grandchild, Benjamin, born to Sheridan and Rick on October 28, 2002. It was such a joy to welcome our bright-eyed grandson, especially with his bright red hair! Cheri and I quickly learned that being grandparents is the best job in the world. During this period Scott was dating Kristen Ely, whom he had met at the University of Colorado. She worked as a medical assistant at the Steadman Clinic in Vail. What's funny is that Scott and Kristen both attended Cherry Creek High School, but she was a year behind him and they didn't know each other then. Eventually, Scott and Kristen got engaged, but Scott wanted to earn his MBA before they got married. He focused on colleges that offered a one-year MBA program and found two options: Notre Dame and the McCombs School of Business at the University of Texas, which is named after Red McCombs, a former owner of the Nuggets. I reached out to Red, who kindly wrote a letter of recommendation for Scott, but Scott's application was still turned down. However, Notre Dame accepted him, so he moved to South Bend, Indiana, in the summer of 2004 and completed his degree in one calendar year.

In the fall of 2004, we sold the Tile Warehouse and our home in Singletree and moved back to Denver. We arrived just in time for the birth of our second grandchild, Addison Mary Whipple, born to Sheridan and Rick on November 15, 2004. Her middle name, Mary, was chosen in honor of Cheri's mom. Now we had two great reasons to be back in Denver: Ben and Addy!

The following year, we had even more reasons to celebrate family. On June 11, 2005, Scott and Kristen tied the knot at Christ Church Denver, with Andrew Klein and Mark Brewer officiating. Kristen is a wonderful person—solid as a rock. Here's a funny story: We held the rehearsal dinner for about seventy-five to eighty people at Ruth's Chris Steak House, so it was a big expense. Almost everyone ordered steak, but my mother, who was always very frugal, opted for chicken!

As Scott and Kristen embarked on their journey together, I was focused on giving back in meaningful ways. One of the initiatives I supported during this time was a charity founded by country music star Garth Brooks called Touch 'Em All, where Major League players made a pledge to support children in the areas of health, education, and inner-city development. The foundation's name has since been changed to Teammates for Kids and expanded to include other sports. Early on, Bo Mitchell, our former chaplain from the Nuggets, was selected to run the foundation.

Scott and Kristen's wedding reception at the Denver Country Club on June 11, 2005, captured just as a rainbow appeared behind them.

Additionally, Bill Bostrom, who was my attorney in Denver, served as the foundation's attorney. Due to my association with both of them, I served on a committee that helped decide which charities received financial support from the foundation.

As a reward for participating athletes, every winter Garth would stage a private concert just for them in Las Vegas. It was an incredible experience. You'd walk into the room and it felt like stepping into the MLB All-Star game. The evening also featured a live auction as a fundraising tool.

One year, while I was sitting in the back of the room during the live auction, Garth—who had played baseball in high school—approached me and said, "Nolan Ryan was my hero when I was playing baseball. They're going to auction off an autographed Nolan Ryan jersey, but I can't bid on it because it would look bad. You buy it, and I'll reimburse you. I don't care how much it costs." When the bidding started, it became clear that a few other Nolan Ryan fans were also in the room. I ended up with the winning bid—$100,000! People came up to me afterward, saying things like, "I didn't know you were such a baseball fan." I never said a word, and

With Garth Brooks, a great guy, at one of his private concerts for the athletes who supported his foundation.

Garth took care of it. In the few times I was around him, it was clear how much he truly cares about others.

In 2005 I worked for Kirk Shiner in a completely different field—water disposal, a critical part of oil and gas operations. When you drill an oil or gas well, some water comes up along with the oil or gas. If you're lucky, it's just a small amount of water, but it can vary from well to well. In some cases, a significant amount of water comes up with the oil or gas. Additionally, there's a process called fracking, where water, along with sand or another material, is pumped down the well to fracture the formation and increase production. Unfortunately, much of this fracking water also comes back up, and it is often contaminated. This "dirty water" is full of hydrocarbons, and you can't just let it run off into the environment—it needs to be disposed of properly.

There are two main ways to dispose of this water. One is called an injection well, which is essentially a nonproducing well where the dirty water is injected back into the ground. The other method is using evaporation pits, where the water is dumped and allowed to evaporate over time, with more water being added as needed. Shiner got involved in this process by building an evaporation pit just over the Colorado line in

Utah. At the time, oil prices were around $100 a barrel, and there were about fifty drilling rigs on the western slope of Colorado. It was a seller's market, with oil companies making so much money that they didn't mind the cost of disposing of the water. I worked for Shiner, visiting companies and helping them bring their dirty water to an evaporation site called the Danish Flats in Utah. That's where the disposal pits were located, and it was a key area for handling the wastewater from the oil and gas operations. Each pit covered about five acres and had to be double-lined with a rubberized liner. Between the two liners we had to install a leak detection system. Building those pits wasn't cheap.

Each truck carried about 130 barrels of water to the evaporation pits, and there were days when we'd offload four hundred trucks in a twenty-four-hour period. We were charging $3 a barrel, so those were big numbers. Once the trucks offloaded, we'd pump the water into the pits and let it evaporate. In the winter, when it was cold and overcast, evaporation was minimal. But in the summer, with the heat and sunshine, we'd see a lot more evaporation. I was probably making $80,000 per year working in sales for Shiner's company, but when oil prices dropped, the oil companies got a lot more selective about how much they were willing to pay to dispose of the water. That's when they started negotiating more aggressively. The company was beginning to feel the financial strain from the situation, but it was nothing compared to the avalanche of problems building in my own finances.

Earlier I talked about my friendship with Brereton Jones. In 2000, five years after leaving the Kentucky governor's office, Brereton partnered with horseman and entrepreneur Tracy Farmer to cofound American Founders Bank, which began in a trailer on a gravel lot in Frankfort. A few years later, they opened a second branch in Frankfort, followed by branches in Shelbyville and Lawrenceburg. Cheri and I were among the top ten investors in the bank. Every time the bank opened a new location, there would be a capital call. To maintain our ownership percentage, Cheri and I borrowed money from Bankers' Bank in Frankfort to purchase more stock; they seemed more than willing to lend it. All of this was happening while I was still working and juggling a busy life. At the time, I didn't fully grasp the risk—we just thought we were being smart and diversified. After all, what's safer than bank stock, right?

American Founders was privately held, so the stock wasn't publicly traded. But among investors, we owned shares in what was considered the fastest-growing bank in the state. American Founders grew to nine branches, but in 2007 the Federal Reserve issued a cease-and-desist order. The reason for our rapid growth was also our downfall: the bank was making one bad loan after another. If someone couldn't repay their loan, they'd just get another loan to make the payments. On top of that, there were some serious irregularities in the accounting practices. If Brereton and Tracy hadn't been such decent people, others involved might have gone to jail over that deal. Meanwhile, Bankers' Bank, which had lent us the money to maintain our equity stake, wanted to be repaid. Around the same time, I had made another bad investment in a housing development in Granby, Colorado, called Grand Elk. It was a stunning resort area with a golf course designed by pro golfer Craig Stadler. A river ran through the valley, perfect for trout fishing. We didn't just buy one residential lot—we bought four. And not just any lots, but the four best (and most expensive) in the development. The only catch? Grand Elk is about sixty miles from the nearest ski resort. There is a small bunny slope nearby, but for people looking for a mountain home, proximity to skiing is a major factor. The lots didn't sell like we'd hoped.

At the time, our financial statement looked solid—otherwise, the banks wouldn't have lent us the money. But everything was leveraged. My income dropped significantly after my buyout from the Nuggets, leaving us with a mountain of interest payments to manage. Starting in about 2007, I struggled to sleep well, knowing I was buried in debt. Between bank investments, the Grand Elk lots, and a handful of other ventures—including some racehorses and their associated veterinary bills—we were heavily invested in nonrevenue-producing assets, all financed with borrowed money. My desire to acquire had grown out of control.

On June 30, 2009, Cheri and I filed for Chapter 7 bankruptcy, having accumulated more than $4.5 million in debt. That included nearly $1 million owed to Bankers' Bank for stock in American Founders Bank, $77,000 in credit card debt, over $258,000 in business loans from American Founders Bank, and nearly $200,000 in costs related to horse training, veterinary care, stables, and boarding. The hardest part for me during that time was having to call my parents and Cheri's dad to tell them what had happened. It was humiliating. Stories about our bankruptcy filing appeared in major newspapers and on television sportscasts. We walked into the courthouse and had to explain everything to the judge, in a room full of strangers. And it wasn't private. There were a hundred other people there, all getting ready to declare bankruptcy, hearing every word that was said.

Then a court representative came to our house and began pointing out our belongings. We were allowed to keep up to $10,000 worth. He'd say things like, "That stool's worth $50. Do you want to keep it or not?" It was awful, truly the worst thing I've ever been through. I even had to surrender my Kentucky Colonels ABA championship ring and my Naismith Memorial Basketball Hall of Fame ring. (I know the guy who sold them, but I don't know who owns them.) But even with how hard it was, we still had our health. We still had our family. We still had our faith. And we still had a few good friends. Once again, the Goldys supported us 100 percent. Barbara came over to help Cheri sort through her jewelry, and she and Bill bought some of our furniture and other belongings we had to sell as part of the bankruptcy. I'm not sure they needed any of it, but it was their way of showing support. It was eye-opening to see who reached out during that time and who didn't. Let's just say our Christmas card list got a lot shorter.

We were broke, starting over from scratch at sixty-one years of age.

One of the most misquoted verses in the Bible is "money is the root of all evil." That's not what it says. The correct wording comes from 1 Timothy, which reads, "for the *love* of money is a root of all kinds of evil."[3] Looking back, I think it was the desire to acquire—to put faith in what we could have and how much we could accumulate—that ultimately led to our downfall. A phrase that appears in the Gospels, "For everyone who exalts himself will be humbled, and he who humbles himself will be exalted," rang true.[4] We were certainly humbled. I believe God puts up barriers to get your attention, and that ordeal was one of those barriers for us.

Since June 30, 2009, we've never borrowed another penny. We have a credit card because there are some things like renting a car that you can't do with a debit card, but I certainly sleep a lot better at night.

The publicity surrounding our financial downfall started to take a toll on us. So, at the invitation of Kirk Shiner we spent about six months at a cabin on his ranch in the small town of McCoy, Colorado, to regroup and heal. During that time, we started attending Sunday services at a local country church. There were probably no more than twenty parishioners, but the people couldn't have been kinder. I have a feeling that some of them knew who I was, but it was never brought up. To them, we were just

With three of our grandkids in 2010, (*from left*) Ben, Brody, and Addy.

neighbors from down the road, living on a ranch and coming to worship. It was just what we needed.

To bring in some much-needed income, I went back to work for Shiner. He'd partnered with engineers at Utah State University who had developed a machine that used heat to evaporate water—a contraption that was supposed to revolutionize the water disposal industry. They had one set up in Danish Flats and were looking to expand, so Shiner hired me as a salesman in New Mexico. My job was to call on oil and gas companies across the state, from Albuquerque to Farmington, and pitch this new water evaporation system.

Cheri and I moved to Santa Fe, where we found a two-bedroom place just a couple of blocks from the square. We enjoyed our time there. The problem was, the machine didn't work. If it had been evaporating clean water, like tap water, it might have been fine. But the water we were dealing with was full of sand and hydrocarbons. When it entered the exhaust system, it would cake over everything and shut the whole thing down. So, there I was, in New Mexico for about six months, trying to sell a product that didn't work and asking potential customers to travel all the way to Danish Flats, Utah, just to see it.

Then the disposal business started to slow down, and the company responded by cutting all the salespeople's salaries in half. The idea was that we'd make up the difference through commissions—which, of course, wasn't happening. The four other salespeople and I joined a company-wide meeting in Salt Lake City with Shiner and the team that had built the machine. Cheri came with me, and on the drive back to Santa Fe, I got a call from my friend Mark Brewer, who was now a pastor at Bel Air Presbyterian Church in Los Angeles. He offered me a job as executive director at Bel Air. I had turned down the same offer from him twice before, but given how bleak things were looking in my sales role, it now had my full attention.

11

Seasons of Change

When Cheri and I flew out to Los Angeles to explore the opportunity with Bel Air Presbyterian Church, everything just felt right. We were ready for a change, something that would recharge us.

The Bel Air campus overlooks the San Fernando Valley, a stunning view. At one point, it was appraised at around $100 million. We were immediately taken by the facility. Plus, Sheridan and Rick had moved to Northern California. Rick worked in downtown San Francisco, and they lived in the East Bay, so the relatively close proximity to family was an added perk to consider.

During that trip, we had dinner with Mark and Carolyn Brewer, Terry and Moncita Botwick, and Brian and Leslie Matthews. Brian ran an investment firm in downtown Los Angeles, and Terry was in the film industry. Brian was about to roll off the church board, and Terry was coming in as board president. What made the dinner even more memorable was learning that Moncita is Rosemary Clooney's daughter, which makes her George Clooney's cousin. The Clooneys are from Maysville, Kentucky.

We also learned that Leslie Matthews is Michael Landon's daughter. Landon, of course, was "Little Joe" on *Bonanza* and the father on *Little House on the Prairie,* one of my favorite shows growing up. But beyond those interesting connections, they were just genuinely great people, and you could feel how passionate they were about Bel Air. After that dinner,

Cheri and I decided I would formally accept Mark's job offer and move to Los Angeles. It felt like God's plan for us.

Once we settled in, Terry Botwick became both a mentor and good friend, while Moncita and Cheri quickly became close friends. We rented an apartment in Marina del Rey, just four blocks from the beach. Even though the church office didn't open until nine o'clock in the morning, I'd arrive by seven to beat traffic and have a little quiet time before the day-to-day operations began.

On my very first day as executive director, my assistant, Joyce Leckie, asked to go to lunch. She offered to resign if I wanted to bring in my own assistant. I told her absolutely not. She had been there for years and was going to be a huge asset. I also became very close with Mark Phillips, the CFO. I rarely made a decision without their input. Joyce helped assess the cultural impact of changes, and Mark handled the financial implications.

Our church had a team of 115 staff members, and a significant part of our work involved running an exceptional preschool. I soon learned that in affluent areas of Los Angeles, the competition is intense. To get into the right high school, a student often needs to have attended the right middle school, which means the right elementary school, kindergarten, and even preschool. The race begins before kids can even tie their own shoes. Shaquille O'Neal's kids attended our preschool, as did children of Gwen Stefani and a member of the rock band KISS.

Because of all the wealthy families and celebrity children who attended, the preschool had really strict rules: no cameras, no recording devices allowed at any events. One year during my tenure, Gwen Stefani's son played Joseph in the Christmas pageant. One of the dads snuck in his cell phone and took a photograph of him in costume, then sold the picture to a British tabloid for $10,000.

We ended up in the preschool director's office—me, the director, and the parents involved. It was the husband who had taken and sold the photograph. He denied everything at first, claiming he'd just shown the picture to a friend, and that the friend must have been the one who sold it. He had a whole story lined up. But then the preschool director told them, "You know this is grounds for expulsion."

The mom immediately turned to her husband and said, "He did it! What do we need to do to make this right?" She threw him under the bus in a second. She wasn't about to let their kid get kicked out of preschool!

In the end, the couple agreed to return the $10,000. Half went to Gwen Stefani, and the other half went to a charity of her choice.

Meanwhile, church life carried on. Sunday was "game day" at Bel Air Presbyterian. We had three services: an early traditional one, another later in the morning with full organ and choir, and a more contemporary service. Plus, there was a Friday night service. I'd get to church around seven o'clock in the morning and start by checking in with the four off-duty LAPD officers we had at each service. Then I'd attend the pre-service meeting with Mark and the music team. Sundays were the heart of it all.

Some well-known people attended our services. Before my tenure, Bel Air was Ronald Reagan's home church. After his presidency, he still had Secret Service protection, and there was only one spot in the sanctuary where he and Nancy could sit, for safety reasons. Unfortunately, it was right under an air conditioning vent. To fix that, a six-foot by two-foot piece of plexiglass was mounted above their seats to block the cold air. It is still there.

The music at our church was always outstanding, thanks to the incredible talent in Los Angeles and our bright, dedicated staff. Many of them had come to Los Angeles hoping to break into the entertainment industry, which is about as long a shot as playing Little League baseball and dreaming of making it to the majors. We also had a drama department that performed short sketches to illustrate Mark's sermons and a media team that created humorous video segments.

One of the real highlights for me was nearly filling the Hollywood Bowl for Easter morning, a yearly tradition. Another was our annual Christmas show, which we held at a theater across the street from the Staples Center. One Christmas, the music department came up with the idea to perform *The Twelve Days of Christmas.* For the "five golden rings" verse, we thought it would be fun to invite Magic Johnson to appear onstage with his championship rings. I actually contacted his representative to pitch the idea, but apparently Magic wasn't interested—he never returned the call.

Beyond the events, one of the biggest highlights of our time in Los Angeles was the friends we made along the way. John and Judy Bedrosian were one such couple. John, a former board member, was a fascinating guy—he started the first company in America to acquire for-profit hospitals and did quite well. Judy and Cheri grew especially close. Every Tuesday, they'd have lunch at Judy's house. Eventually they decided to do

Of all Cheri's paintings, this one is my favorite. It's a Kentucky Wildcat, of course.

something creative with that time. Judy had a stash of art supplies in her garage, so they started painting—completely self-taught.

The Bedrosians had a friend who owned an art gallery in Palm Springs, and Cheri ended up doing a small show there with about eight or ten of her paintings. I remember her telling me that the first piece she ever sold was an 8-by-10-inch painting of a giraffe for $1,800! I've often wondered how far Cheri's art career might have gone if she had started earlier, taken lessons, and pursued it more seriously. To this day, the Bedrosians still have a house in Snowmass, Colorado, and every summer, Moncita, Judy, and Cheri get together there for a week or two.

While my work in Los Angeles kept me busy, life outside of the City of Angels carried on. Family kept me grounded, no matter how far apart we were. Sheridan's husband, Rick, had taken a job in Northern California, and they were living in nearby Danville. We would occasionally drive up to visit them. Around this time, we received news that my dad had fallen in the shower and broken his ankle. He and my mom lived in Hot Springs, Arkansas, near my sister, Kathi, and her husband, Steve. Mom had been my dad's primary caregiver since he survived a heart attack about three years earlier, so he was already in a weakened state. His recovery from the fall required a stay in a rehabilitation center, where he could be closely monitored. While visiting him at the rehab center, my mom contracted a serious staph infection and had to be hospitalized. Cheri and I caught a flight the next day to be with her.

One day, Cheri and my sister had gone out for coffee or something, and I was sitting alone outside my mom's hospital room. The doctor stepped out, looked at me, and said, "You know, we could operate, but it probably wouldn't be successful. And it would put her through a lot of pain. Or, we could put her in hospice."

I didn't know what to say. I've always hated being in hospitals—and especially conversations around death and dying. I stammered a bit, but eventually managed, "It's up to her. I don't think she wants to go through that."

The doctor replied, "Well, I'll go ask her. Do you want to come in with me?"

"No," I said. "I don't want to be part of that conversation."

He went in to speak with my mom. When he came back out, he said, "No, she does not want to go through with the operation."

With Bill Walton (*left*) and Julius Erving on our way to the Naismith Memorial Basketball Hall of Fame's 2019 induction ceremony.

After that, I walked into her room. She looked at me, smiled faintly, and said, "Chicken." She knew how much I hated hospitals, how much I dreaded anything like this. Mom passed away about three days later. Dad, who never left the rehab center, passed about nine months after her. They were both eighty-four. I miss them both every day.

When Mark Brewer decided to leave Los Angeles to pastor another church in Denver, we followed about four months later, in 2014. We moved back to be closer to our grandchildren—Scott and Kristen's kids: Brody, Greyson, and Henry. Sheridan and Rick had also relocated from California to Denver with their kids, Ben and Addy, so for the first time in years our entire family was finally in one place!

I returned to work with Shiner for a while but eventually started my own water disposal business with partners called Bluegrass Water. Several months into that new venture, in September of 2015, I received a meaningful honor: I was named one of fourteen inductees into the inaugural Hall of Honor at Batavia High School. The class included notable figures such as Kenny Anderson, Craig Sager, longtime Batavia High School social studies teacher and basketball coach Jim Roberts, Batavia mayor Jeff Schielke—the longest-serving mayor in the city's history—and Donald Kramer, who served the Batavia community for over thirty years as a deputy, sergeant, lieutenant, and sheriff. "Batavia is more than just memories," I said during my induction speech. "Growing up in this blue-collar, hardworking, Godfearing community, you learn some very valuable lessons. You learn character, a good work ethic, and you learn how people should treat one another. And for that, I'll always be thankful for Batavia."

About a year and a half later, I found myself back in Batavia, this time for a more somber event. I had been asked to speak at a celebration of life held at Batavia High School for my childhood friend Craig Sager, who passed away from leukemia in December of 2016.

Craig and my brother, Greg, were best friends growing up. But what I remember most about Craig is how loyal he remained to Greg's family, even after Greg passed away. Whenever he was in Chicago covering a Bulls game, he'd always reach out to Paula—my sister-in-law—and invite her, along with my niece and nephew, Kate and Rob. He'd say, "I'll leave tickets for you. Come see the game, and we'll have dinner afterward." Paula and the kids often took him up on it.

In 2019, Cheri and I celebrated our fiftieth wedding anniversary in the Dominican Republic.

Craig even did something I've always dreamed of but never had the chance to do: sing "Take Me Out to the Ball Game" at Wrigley Field. Sager went once and made sure to invite Paula and the kids to join him there.

These trips back to my hometown proved to be a meaningful turning point. Not long after Cheri and I returned to Denver, I decided to sell Bluegrass Water. I was briefly retired when I got a call from my long-time attorney, J. Bruce Miller. He'd been talking with Joe Steier, head of Signature HealthCARE in Louisville and a big sports fan. Bruce told him he believed NBA expansion was imminent, so Joe pulled together a group of investors. That day, Cheri and I were planning to drive back to Denver from Louisville, but before we hit the road we stopped by Big Spring Country Club to meet with Bruce, Joe, and Sherm Henderson, a local businessman. That's when they offered me the position of president of NBA2Lou—an effort to bring an NBA team to Louisville if the league expanded. After conferring with Cheri, I accepted the offer and we split our time between Denver and a furnished apartment in Louisville.

I started speaking all over Kentucky to drum up interest from potential investors, and the support was strong. One of the first things I did was call NBA Commissioner Adam Silver to ask if I could come to New York to meet with him. He said, "I'm not taking any meetings on expansion. I'd love to see you—you can come and visit—but I'm not talking about expansion." That slowed our momentum. What really brought things to a halt, though, was the COVID-19 pandemic, which hit in the spring of 2020. For about six months, Cheri and I barely left our apartment except to go to the grocery store.

The NBA2Lou team provided me with a nice salary, and the original plan was to split my time between Louisville and Denver. But after paying for two residences and spending more time in Louisville than expected, we ended up living there full-time from the start of COVID until 2022, working on NBA2Lou. Unfortunately, it never came to fruition. The project basically stalled. The investors had certain financial benchmarks they needed to meet, and while we made some progress, the momentum had slowed so much that Joe Steier and I didn't feel right asking for more money. NBA2Lou still technically exists, but it has been put on hold. If Louisville ever has a real shot again at NBA expansion, we'll certainly pick things back up—but it looks like Las Vegas and Seattle are the odds-on favorites if the league decides to expand. I'd say the chances of expansion are about even.

Teammates again! Mike Pratt and me hosting our radio show at the ESPN Louisville studios.

I've always believed that Louisville deserves a professional basketball team. In hindsight, John Y. Brown probably made the right decision selling the Kentucky Colonels during my playing era, but if you look at the Nuggets, Spurs, Pacers, and Nets—the four ABA teams that joined the NBA—they've all done incredibly well. I thought the 1975 Colonels were the best team in basketball. If we could've kept that roster intact and entered the NBA, I truly believe the Colonels would've been a very successful franchise.

One of the things that kept us in Louisville after NBA2Lou was put on pause was my morning radio show with Mike Pratt on ESPN Louisville. I really enjoyed that. Our show was from ten o'clock to noon. We'd get to the station around nine o'clock, supposedly for show prep—but mostly we just relived our Kentucky careers. It was a blast.

The run lasted until Mike got so sick from cancer that he had to step away. He eventually passed away in June 2022. Mike truly lived by the Golden Rule. He treated everybody the way that he wanted to be treated. He always made time for people. I miss him a lot.

During a celebration of Mike's life that was held at Memorial Coliseum, I shared a story from our senior year at UK with those gathered to honor his memory. There were four or five couples—boosters—who traveled to all of our away games. The night before each game, Coach Rupp would host the traveling party and a few others in his hotel room. At the time, most towns in the SEC were dry, so it fell to our trainer, Claude Vaughan, to supply the refreshments for these gatherings. It was an unofficial part of his job. He'd pack a separate suitcase containing a bottle or two of bourbon and whatever else was needed for the evening.

One night, we were in Oxford, Mississippi. Mike and I were walking down the hotel hallway when we noticed that Claude's door was slightly ajar. Curious, we peeked inside. Claude wasn't there, but sitting on the bed was the open suitcase—with the booze inside, including a six-pack of beer. Mike grabbed the six-pack, and we quickly headed back to our room. Not ten minutes later, there was a knock at the door. It was Claude.

He said, "I know you guys took that six-pack. Where is it?"

We played dumb: "Claude, what are you talking about? We don't know anything about a six-pack."

But he wasn't buying it. He searched the whole room—the closet, the bathtub, under the bed—everywhere. But he couldn't find it.

Eventually he gave up and left. Turns out, Mike had come up with a clever hiding spot. He'd taken the lid off the back of the toilet tank and stashed the six-pack inside.

Claude never found it. And of course, after the game the next night, Mike and I may have enjoyed one or two of those well-hidden beers.

About eight months after that celebration of life ceremony, Mike's jersey was raised to the rafters of Rupp Arena in his honor. His wife,

Marcia, asked me to participate in the ceremony. He'll always be remembered among the greats.

After Mike passed, I began doing the radio show with Louie Rabaut. Later that year, Cheri and I relocated to Denver, but I continued hosting the show remotely from my kitchen table for about a year before stepping away.

Since returning to Denver, I've enjoyed having more time with Cheri and our family. Nothing matters to me more than family. We're five minutes from Scott and his family, and about ten minutes from Sheridan and hers. Every Thursday night we have dinner with Sheridan and Rick. Their kids, Ben and Addy, are both in college now, but we've kept that standing dinner tradition going.

Ben and Addy aren't involved in sports anymore, but when they were, Cheri and I attended as many of their events as we could. In 2015, when Ben was twelve, his Denver-based baseball team participated in a traveling league and competed in the twelve-year-old tournament in Cooperstown, New York. Ben had a great tournament and hit several home runs. We even bought Cheri a T-shirt that read, "My grandson hit a home run in Cooperstown." It was a special trip. While there we visited the National Baseball Hall of Fame and Museum. I remember standing next to Ernie Banks's plaque with Ben. That meant a lot to me, since Ernie was my hero growing up. When I was Ben's age, I thought I'd be the shortstop for the Chicago Cubs. I even bought a Cubs hat at the Hall of Fame that day, and I still have it.

After leaving Cooperstown, we drove to Springfield, Massachusetts, to visit the Naismith Memorial Basketball Hall of Fame. Fran Judkins, the vice president of Hall of Fame relations, treated us to lunch at the Hall's restaurant and led a private tour for Cheri, Sheridan, Rick, Ben, Addy, and me. During the tour, Fran pointed to a wall and told Ben and Addy, "Since the invention of basketball by Dr. Naismith, over 2 billion people have played, coached, or officiated the game. And your grandfather is one of only 412 people [at the time] inducted into the Basketball Hall of Fame." I'm not sure how much that moment registered with the kids, but it sure hit me. I always knew it was an honor. I just didn't realize how rare it really was.

In 2021, Addy was a really strong high school volleyball player. She played for a club called the Colorado Juniors that traveled all over the

In November 2020, my grandson Ben Whipple signed his commitment to pitch for the University of Hawai'i Rainbow Warriors baseball team. *From left:* Sheridan, Addy, Ben, and Rick.

country for tournaments in cities like Detroit, Omaha, and Kansas City. That year, the national tournament was in Las Vegas. These volleyball tournaments are massive. You might see a hundred courts in one convention center, with matches going on everywhere. Addy's team qualified for the national tournament, and while we were having lunch with her in the food court, I spotted UK volleyball coach Craig Skinner walking by. He was scouting players. He had been a guest on the radio show I did with Mike Pratt, and I wanted to say hello and thank him for being on our show. But when I mentioned it, Addy got super nervous. She thought I was trying to get him to watch her play! I had to reassure her, "No, honey, I'm just going to say hi."

Living in Denver as a retiree enables me to watch Scott and Kristen's boys grow up, which means a lot to me. Cheri and I make it to as many of their baseball and basketball games as we can. Now, I fully support youth sports, but I'm often struck by how much money is involved. For example, my grandson Henry is nine years old at present. He and his teammates have two full baseball uniforms each, head to toe, and they travel for games. Some parents and coaches get really worked up. We went to a game a couple of weeks ago where the opposing coach was ejected for arguing with the umpire. These are nine-year-olds, and their coach is getting thrown out of the game! There's just so much pressure on winning instead of focusing on the kids having fun. Many parents seem to have dreams of scholarships or professional careers for their children, but that's such a long shot. I'd love to see more emphasis on just letting kids play and enjoy themselves, especially at this age. Once they get to high school and scholarships are more realistic, I get it. But right now, it should be kids playing, learning, and having a good time.

One of my favorite memories with my grandkids was attending the first game of the 2023 NBA championship series between the Nuggets and the Miami Heat at Ball Arena. Thanks to Lisa Johnson—my former assistant during my time with the Nuggets—I had four seats just four rows behind the Nuggets bench.

The only problem? I was in a real bind trying to decide who to bring, since I have five grandchildren. But just a few days before the game, the Nuggets called and told me they had two additional courtside seats available. All they asked in return was that I do a pregame meet and greet with some of the season ticket holders. That solved everything. I now had six seats and could bring all five grandkids.

The Nuggets even sent a car to pick us up, and off we went to the game. Since Henry and Greyson were the youngest, we decided Henry would sit courtside with me during the first half, and Greyson would take that seat in the second half. While I was off doing the meet and greet, I handed my credit card to my oldest grandson, Ben, and told him, "Go grab something to eat, and you can stop by the souvenir stand to pick something out."

I figured they'd get a hot dog and a Coke at a concession stand. Instead, they went to a sit-down restaurant inside Ball Arena. When they returned, they were all wearing brand-new Nuggets jerseys. Ben had charged nearly $1,000 to my card. That was the last time I ever gave the grandkids my credit card! But honestly, it's one of my favorite memories, sharing that unforgettable night, the first game of the NBA Finals, with all five of my grandkids. What a moment.

Although I wasn't connected to the Nuggets when they won the 2023 NBA championship, it was still a great thrill for me. I've always been a loyal ABA supporter—both as a participant and a fan—so seeing a former ABA team win it all, even after so many years, meant a lot. I know most people don't really make that connection anymore, but I certainly did. I felt proud—not just because it was a former ABA team, but because it was a team I had both played for and coached. That made it even more special.

I've met several of the current Nuggets players as of this writing, including Nikola Jokić. We've had a few conversations—not about basketball, but about horse racing. He's a big fan of trotters and owns several horses back in Serbia. In fact, when he won his first MVP, then–Nuggets coach Michael Malone flew over there to present the trophy. Jokić came jogging up in a cart, driving a trotter at the barn. That's how Malone gave him the award. He reminds me a bit of myself early in my career. The day after the season ends, he's already back home. He doesn't spend much of his free time in Denver. Even after the championship, he was eager to leave; he wasn't thrilled that the victory parade took so long. He just wanted to get back to his horses.

But honestly, I was happiest for the people in the Nuggets front office. I still know a lot of them from my time with the organization. For them to finally experience a championship, it was very special. These moments are rare. Like I mentioned earlier, with the Colonels, I always felt we should have won two or three championships—but we only got one. So, I know how hard it is to reach the top.

With the only two other UK men's basketball players ever to score more than two thousand points in their careers: Kenny "Sky" Walker (*left*) and Jack "Goose" Givens.

While supporting our grandkids' sports endeavors keeps us busy on evenings and weekends, I've stayed active in other parts of life, too, especially in the horse business. My son, Scott, and I have a partnership called Arapahoe Thoroughbreds. We've got some mares in Kentucky and one racehorse we're especially excited about named Kanojo. In the fall of 2024, Cheri and I drove to Des Moines and watched her win a $100,000 stakes race in just her second start. So, these days, it's all about grandkids and horses—and I couldn't be happier.

But as much joy as this season of my life brings, it has also come with a few scary moments that remind me how quickly things can change. In 2024, my grandson Brody had a serious accident that could have been devastating. One afternoon, he was riding his skateboard through the neighborhood—without a helmet, of course—when his mom, Kristen, received a call from a neighbor. Brody had been found unconscious in the street. He'd fallen and hit his head, apparently while coming downhill. Kristen called us right away.

There's a hospital just a few minutes from us, and the ambulance took him there. Kristen and her dad were with him, and Cheri and I rushed over as soon as we could. Scott, Brody's dad, was in Jacksonville, Florida, attending quarterly meetings for the mortgage company where he works as a chief financial officer.

It was a scary situation. Brody had no memory of the fall and was drifting in and out of consciousness. The doctors quickly determined he needed more specialized care and arranged to transfer him to Children's Hospital Colorado in Aurora. They initially planned to airlift him by helicopter, but severe weather made that impossible. Instead, he was taken by ambulance later that night.

Meanwhile, Scott was stranded in Jacksonville, desperate to get home and overwhelmed with worry. The following morning, the doctors discovered enough swelling on Brody's brain to warrant emergency surgery. They performed a procedure to relieve the pressure by removing a small section of his skull—about the size of a quarter—just above his left ear, where he'd hit his head. It was terrifying for all of us.

Because of hospital restrictions, only a few of us were allowed in his room at a time, so we took turns while the rest waited in the lobby. Scott finally made it back from Florida that afternoon. Mark and Carolyn Brewer came to visit, and we all gathered to pray for Brody's recovery.

Remarkably, he began to heal very quickly. Even the doctors were amazed. Brody was in great shape for a fifteen-year-old, and that helped. He was out of the hospital within a few days. The hardest part afterward was trying to keep him from overexerting himself because he felt so good so soon. We truly feel his recovery was an answer to prayer, especially considering the severity of his injury. It feels like a miracle.

These days, Brody is doing great. He's interested in aviation and is a member of the local Civil Air Patrol. He's already had several flight lessons, and every six months or so he gets to go up in a small single-engine plane. His dream is to become an airline pilot. With a brain bleed, there's a mandatory five-year waiting period before you can get a pilot's license. That's been tough for him, but he's only a sophomore in high school, so five years will pass quickly.

Epilogue

As of this writing, the last time the Kentucky Wildcats won an NCAA men's basketball championship was in 2012, when Cheri, Sheridan, Ben, and I attended the Final Four in New Orleans. On the Sunday between the semifinals and the championship game, we attended the Naismith Memorial Basketball Hall of Fame breakfast. When we arrived, we noticed Bill Walton sitting at a table with four open seats. I've known Bill since my Nuggets days, and he used to have bright red hair before it turned gray. When he saw Ben, who has bright red hair, he looked up to us and said, "Sit here!" Then he pointed to the seat next to him and told Ben, "You sit next to me."

After breakfast with Bill, we headed into a small auditorium, where Naismith Hall of Fame officials announced that year's Hall of Fame class. Ben sat right next to Bill. During the event, they also presented the Bob Cousy Award, given to the top point guard in college basketball.

Cousy wasn't there in person, but they played a video of him explaining what makes a great point guard. He said something like, "You have to get the ball to your teammates where they can succeed. Think pass first, shoot second."

When the video ended, Bill leaned over to Ben and whispered, "Ben, don't believe all that BS. Shoot it every time you get it."

From that moment on, Ben and Bill became fast friends. Bill couldn't have been kinder to Ben that weekend.

Cheri and I (*center*) attended the 2020 Naismith Memorial Basketball Hall of Fame induction ceremony with (*from left*) Enola and Artis Gilmore and Judy and Louie Dampier.

While I'm on the topic of the Naismith Hall of Fame, one person I believe deserves to be enshrined but isn't is my old coach Doug Moe. Doug grew up in New York and attended Erasmus Hall High School before being recruited to play for Frank McGuire at the University of North Carolina. He was a two-time First-Team All-ACC selection and earned All-American honors in 1961. In fact, my father-in-law, Virgil, saw him play in college once and said he was something special.

Unfortunately, Doug was accused of having contact with a known gambler and was banned from playing in the NBA. Around that same time, other players like Connie Hawkins and Roger Brown were also accused of gambling-related issues. Both ended up starting their pro careers in the ABA and later made it to the Naismith Hall of Fame.

Doug, on the other hand, had to go overseas and became a star in Italy. By the time he returned to play in the ABA, his knees were basically shot. He was playing bone-on-bone. Still, in one poll he was voted among the top thirty players in ABA history.[1]

After his playing days, Doug went on to have a long and successful coaching career. He coached first with the San Antonio Spurs, then with the Denver Nuggets, where he won 628 games and was named NBA Coach of the Year in 1988. He never won a championship—largely because the Lakers were always in the way—but his impact on the game was undeniable. Whether it's as a player, coach, or contributor, there should be a place for Doug Moe in the Naismith Memorial Basketball Hall of Fame.

When people see how tall I am, the inevitable question comes up: *Did you play basketball?* Then comes the follow-up: *Who did you play for?* And I don't say the Kentucky Colonels or the Denver Nuggets—I say the University of Kentucky. That always gets a reaction: *You played at Kentucky?* There's a weight to that name, a tradition that commands attention.

College basketball programs come and go. No one stays on top for long. Duke wasn't consistently solid until Coach K arrived. Indiana was great under Bobby Knight but hasn't been the same since. UCLA was unstoppable under Coach Wooden, but they've faded a bit in recent years. But Kentucky, along with Kansas and North Carolina, has been a consistently elite program from the beginning. Being part of that tradition is a real honor.

Sure, Kentucky has had its ups and downs, but college basketball is never going to be the same. With Name, Image, and Likeness (NIL) and the transfer portal, things have changed dramatically—and I'm all for players getting paid. For years, the NCAA made a fortune off these so-called amateur athletes. It never sat right with me that some parents couldn't afford to travel and see their kids play. So, I fully support athletes earning money off their athletic ability. That said, there have to be some guardrails. The NCAA dropped the ball by failing to build a workable system beyond full-ride athletic scholarships. Instead, it clung to the old model and rolled the dice in court. That gamble collapsed in 2021 with the Supreme Court's decision in *NCAA v. Alston.* Although the case technically focused on education-related benefits, it weakened the legal foundation of amateurism and made it risky for the NCAA to limit athlete compensation at all. Together with new state NIL laws, the ruling set off a rush of deals and endorsements. Now, everything feels out of control, and if anyone tries to rein it in, there will be lawsuits waiting. The lack of a clear framework from the start is going to hurt college basketball in the long run.

I've been lucky to be the 'Y' in Kentucky at a few UK basketball games. It's always such a fun experience. (Courtesy of the *Lexington Herald-Leader,* photograph by Mark Cornelison.)

But my school? Kentucky is in a great spot. In this new landscape, the "haves" will only gain more advantages, while the "have nots" will risk falling further behind. That doesn't guarantee that every major program will succeed, but it does mean they'll hold an edge in recruiting from both high schools and the transfer portal. Kentucky has the facilities, the NIL support, and the name recognition. It's built to thrive.

The one-and-done era may have dominated for a while, but now, with players bouncing between three or four schools and staying for five or six years, the winning formula is going to be a mix. You need a few young stars who can play right away, but you also need veterans who know how to win, much like the roster of the 2025 Houston Cougars, the runners-up in that year's NCAA men's national basketball championship game. Because of that, I think there are only going to be seven or eight teams each year that truly have a shot at the national championship.

Looking back, I still can't believe I ended up at UK. Honestly, it felt like divine intervention. I was a late bloomer—a real long shot to make it there—so my story is proof that even those who don't shine early on can still rise. I hope it inspires boys and girls who aren't born athletic stars. The program already had high school All-Americans and All-State players on board, and I was the twelfth freshman to sign that year. I didn't know it then, but the decision to attend UK completely shaped the rest of my life. I met Cheri there and I played for Coach Rupp, who really pushed me and made me a much better player. And I had the incredible opportunity to play for one of the top college programs in the country. I will say this—if there had been a transfer portal back then, probably ten out of the twelve of us freshmen would've left, based on how we were treated. But I'm glad there wasn't, I'm glad I stuck it out.

The game of basketball itself has definitely changed since my era. In college, the NBA, and probably high school, too, everything now revolves around the three-point shot. I think the game has lost some balance, but I believe it'll come back around. Back in the day, when the ball went into the low post, if the player was a threat there was an immediate double-team. Now? That rarely happens. Teams are so worried about kickouts for open threes that they don't even help in the post anymore.

The other day, I was flipping through the media guide from my rookie year with the Colonels. That season, we had seven stretches where we played three nights in a row, and at one point we played four nights straight: first at home against New York, then in Indiana to play the Pacers, followed by a game in Norfolk against the Squires, and back home in Louisville to host the Memphis Pros. Playing three nights in a row wasn't fun, but we did it. That's just the way it was.

Nowadays in the NBA? A guy gets a hangnail and he's out for a week or ten days. They've got "load management." To me, the biggest change in the NBA is how soft the players have become. When we traveled, it was coach class. We stayed in motels. Our per diem was $12 per day. I know things cost more now, but today's players fly charter, stay in five-star hotels, and get over $100 a day in per diem. I don't know why, since the team feeds them constantly anyway.

I might sound like the "get off my lawn" guy here, but I think the game of basketball is evolving, and not always for the better. There's barely a midrange game anymore. But that, too, will swing back. Basketball is still a great sport. Some say NBA players have too much power now—and maybe they do. Management often gives in because they don't want a star demanding a trade. But despite all the noise around the game, it's still basketball at its core. People might try to mess it up, but in the end, they can't.

My son, Scott, and I pose by the statue of Ernie Banks during a trip to Wrigley Field in August 2023.

Throughout my playing career, one of the biggest blessings was having had a great high school coach who made sure I understood the basics. You've got to learn how to dribble, how to pass, how to defend, the core skills. Today, I think too many young players are so physically gifted that the coaches around them often skip over teaching the game itself. They rely too much on athleticism.

For any young person serious about basketball, my advice is this: learn how to *play* the game. Become strong in the fundamentals, because no matter how talented you are, sooner or later—whether it's in grade school, high school, or college—you'll go up against someone just as physically gifted. And when that happens, your understanding of the game and your mastery of the fundamentals will set you apart.

Another thing I've learned is the importance of having a sense of humor in life and remembering that, at the end of the day, basketball is just a game. Now, when the game was on and I was out there competing, I was serious and gave it everything I had. But off the court—in the locker room, with friends, with family—we knew how lucky we were to be playing a kids' game for a living. We weren't splitting the atom; we were playing basketball. And it was a lot more enjoyable when you allowed yourself to have fun doing it. I think that's one of the biggest differences between my playing days and now—for a few reasons. First, today's NBA players are making so much money. And second, with social media and all the constant criticism out there, it just doesn't seem like a lot of guys are truly enjoying the game.

We had fun. And for us, fun meant going out there and kicking somebody's tail. But even with that edge, I always understood there's a time to be serious and a time not to be, and I think I managed to find that balance.

A couple of weeks ago, the message at church was about legacy, and I thought the pastor, Craig Smith, made a powerful point. He said, *"Your legacy isn't as important as how you pursue it."* That really stuck with me. For me, my legacy will always be basketball. It's the one thing I was ever truly good at. But what matters more is how you live while building that legacy. How you treat people. What kind of friend and teammate you are. Whether you try to do the right thing. What kind of parent and spouse you become. How people feel after they spend time with you. I just hope, in the end, that I was as good at those things as I was at basketball.

Jennifer DiBiase, the daughter of our longtime friends the Goldys, once said something that stayed with me: "When I think about you," she told me, "the thing I remember most is how you always pay attention to me." She went on to say, "Whenever we're talking, you sit down so your height doesn't overwhelm me, and you really look at me. You're not scanning the room or distracted. You're listening, really listening, and that makes me feel seen."

I didn't realize how much that mattered until she said it out loud. Her words reminded me that presence—simple and undivided attention—is a quiet kind of legacy, but a lasting one.

I'm closing in on my eighth decade of life, so I'm pretty set in my routine. I get up every morning, check my emails, and then I read. First, the *Thoroughbred Daily News* to catch up on everything happening in the world of horse racing. Then I check ESPN, and after that I read Fox News to stay on top of current events—all on my computer. After that, I do my Bible reading and prayers. Then I get on the treadmill for an hour. I try to walk three miles five or six times a week—and I don't lollygag. I get those three miles in under an hour.

In the afternoon, I usually watch horse racing on the television. Or sometimes I'll watch an old *Andy Griffith* episode. I also love to read. My favorite author is Dick Francis, a British steeplechase jockey and crime writer who passed away in 2010. He wrote a number of mystery novels, most of which were set against the backdrop of racetracks. Francis published a new book every year throughout much of his career, and for many years his latest mystery was one of my favorite Christmas presents.

In addition to mysteries, I also enjoy reading history, especially about wars. I'm not entirely sure why I have such a fascination with that, but it might be because I lived through the Vietnam War. I particularly enjoy reading about World War I, World War II, and especially the Civil War.

I'm currently reading a historical fiction series called *The Bregdan Chronicles* by Ginny Dye. There are about twenty books in the series, and I've read them all. The story follows a family living in Virginia and explores their experiences during and after the Civil War.

At night, Cheri and I usually watch a show—something on Paramount+ or Netflix—or I'll tune into a sporting event. But more than anything, we love watching our grandkids compete. Whether it's basketball or baseball, there's nothing better than seeing them out there doing what they love.

And if you'll allow me a moment, I'd like to brag about them a little. Our oldest grandson is Benjamin, Sheridan and Rick's son. He was quite

In 2025, my grandsons and I attended a Cubs-Rockies game at Coors Field and caught up with the Rockies radio crew in the press box. *From left:* Rockies radio announcer Jack Corrigan, Henry, Greyson, Brody, and play-by-play announcer Jerry Schemmel. Jerry called Nuggets games when I coached.

a baseball player growing up. We had the chance to travel all over the country with his teams, from California to Florida and everywhere in between. It was really fun to follow him.

I had hoped he'd become a basketball player, but he was much better at baseball. In fact, Ben received a baseball scholarship to the University of Hawai'i, but after injuring his arm his playing career ended. He transferred to the University of Colorado to be closer to family and friends, and after graduating he landed a job in Austin, Texas, with a financial services company.

When he moved to Austin, he invited me to join him on the two-day drive from Denver. We had a great time. I had prepared a little speech to give him with some life advice, things to do and not do. But about two minutes in, I realized he was more prepared for adulthood than I ever was, so I just shut up and enjoyed the ride.

All five of our grandchildren are excellent students. They must've taken after Cheri's side of the family. I always tease them when they tell me about their report cards. I say, "You know, I never got a B," implying I got straight As. Truth is, it was more like straight Cs or worse. But they're all doing great.

Addison is Sheridan and Rick's daughter, and she's just like her mom: laser-focused. When she decides to pursue something, she doesn't stop until she achieves it. She's majoring in international business and psychology in college, and she's already been on several mission trips with teams, but without any family members. She's been to Mexico, Thailand, Africa, and India. Her faith is important to her, and we're so proud of her.

Brody is Scott and Kristen's oldest. He's our worker bee. Since he was about twelve, he's been doing yard work and snow removal for most of the neighbors. If you give him a job, he's a perfectionist; he doesn't rush through it like most kids might. He's not really an athlete, which I admire. He gave baseball and basketball a try, but it just wasn't for him. I respect that he didn't keep going with it just because others expected him to. Instead, he's found a real passion for automobiles and aviation. His goal is to become a commercial airline pilot, and with his work ethic I have no doubt he'll get there.

Our fourth grandchild, Greyson, is Scott and Kristen's second, and he's probably the most like me. He's extremely competitive, a better athlete at this age than I was. He's great at basketball, baseball, football, and golf. You name it. But once the game is over, he moves on. One time I asked him the score of a baseball game he'd played in, and he just said, "They had a lot, and we had a little." Personality-wise, we're very similar. He's a solid student but he tends to do exactly what's required. When he was in elementary school, they invited him to join a gifted program, and he said, "No, I think I'm good where I am." That's exactly what I would have done.

Then there's the youngest, Henry. He might just be the brightest of all the grandkids. Like his dad, Scott, he has almost a photographic memory, and his math skills are off the charts. He's also competitive. We have a little space under the stairs we call the cubbyhole. When he'd spend the night, we'd set up a blow-up mattress in there. He'd bring his books, stuffed animals, a clock, and a lantern, and that's where he'd sleep. On a recent visit, though, he told us, "I think I'm ready to move into the guest room." We don't have any little boys anymore.

For Cheri and me, it's truly a blessing. We have a close relationship with all five of our grandkids, and so far they're all growing into remarkable young people.

Cheri and I are truly blessed with a great family. *Back row, from left:* Scott, Brody, me, Ben, and Rick. *Front row, from left:* Kristen, Greyson, Henry, Cheri, Addy, and Sheridan. Thanksgiving 2025.

When it comes to my spiritual journey, I honestly don't know how people get through life without faith. Everyone is going to face tough times. Everyone is going to make mistakes. I remember hearing the late American radio broadcaster Paul Harvey once say, "Failure is not falling down. Failure is not getting back up." You get up, dust yourself off, and keep going. Every time I've made it through failure, I've come out happier on the other side.

But for me—and for Cheri, and thankfully our whole family—faith has always been our foundation. Like anyone, my walk of faith hasn't always been steady. Sometimes it felt rock solid; other times, not so much. Back when I was playing, we had games on Saturday nights or were constantly traveling, so getting to church regularly was tough. But now? I think I'm happier than I've ever been—and my faith is stronger than it's ever been. This past Easter, our whole family filled an entire pew at our home church, Mission Hills in Littleton. That felt like such a blessing. We never pushed faith on our kids, but they saw how much it meant to us. And now, it means something to them, too. It brings me so much joy to see our grandkids going to church and growing in their own faith. It's a beautiful thing.

Acknowledgments

It took a great team behind the scenes to help Doug Brunk and me get this book across the finish line. I want to start by thanking the dedicated staff at the University Press of Kentucky, especially director Ashley Runyon, for the guidance and support along the way.

We're also grateful to the folks who helped us track down photographs: Deb Moore from UK Athletics; Brian Simms at the *Lexington Herald-Leader;* Sarah Coblenz and Jason Flahardy at the University of Kentucky Special Collections Research Center; Lloyd "Pink" Gardner, who was the trainer for the ABA Kentucky Colonels back in the day; and Mark Gordon, who took some great shots of me during my playing days with the Colonels.

A big thank-you to Hannah Storm of ESPN for writing the foreword—it means a lot. Her father, Mike Storen, was my general manager with the Kentucky Colonels.

I also want to thank my wife, Cheri, and our children, Sheridan and Scott, for reading early versions of the manuscript and giving us ideas for things to add. And a special nod of appreciation to our longtime family friend Barbara Goldy, who reminded me of some stories I hadn't thought about in years.

And last but not least, thanks to Doug Brunk. I knew this project would take a lot of time and effort, but his professionalism made it more fun than I ever expected.

Dan Issel

The older I get, the more I've come to appreciate how life has a way of coming full circle. Dan Issel was the very first person I interviewed back in 2012 for my first book, *Wildcat Memories: Inside Stories from Kentucky Basketball Greats.* Working with him again to tell his story has been a real honor, and I'm grateful he trusted me to be part of it. The enthusiasm he showed throughout our collaboration was infectious.

In *Man's Search for Meaning,* Viktor Frankl—the neurologist and Holocaust survivor—writes, "The meaning of your life is to help others find the meaning of theirs." If this book holds any meaning, may it find its way to Dan, and to those closest to him.

I was fortunate to have a small but mighty crew in my corner throughout this project, including my mother, Genevieve Brunk; my brother, Bob Brunk; my sister-in-law, Debra Isaacs; my mother-in-law, Barbara Goran; and the rest of my extended family.

Thanks as well to many friends who cheered me on, including Rob Bolton, Tim Boyle, Dean and Ruth Cook, Kevin Cook, Todd Cook, Scott Courts, Jack Givens, Dave Good, Scott Farmelant, George Fletcher, Pernell and Tracey Francis, John Huang, Bruce Jancin, Mark Koger, Rick and Lisa Lofgren, Elizabeth Mechcatie, Dean and Marcia Nelson, Wayne and Alice Rogers, Terry Rudd, and Dave Weiner.

Most of all, my greatest supporter during this journey was my wife, Vickie Brunk. I'm grateful for her encouragement and support every single day.

Doug Brunk

Notes

2. Turning Point

1. Arvid Koontz, "Batavia Dethrones Sycamore as Little Seven Champions, 75–61," *DeKalb (Ill.) Daily Chronicle,* February 12, 1965.

2. Ralph Leo, "Looking for a Little David in Basketball? Could Be Batavia!" *Chicago Tribune,* February 25, 1965.

3. John Leusch, "One Little David Left: It's Batavia," *Chicago Tribune,* March 8, 1965.

4. Michael Hess, "Batavia Trips Elgin in Sectional Battle," *Arlington Heights (Ill.) Daily Herald,* March 18, 1965.

5. Cooper Rollow, "Batavia Mowed Down, 77 to 74, in Overtime," *Chicago Tribune,* March 13, 1965.

6. "Issel Saves Batavia with Second to Go," *DeKalb (Ill.) Chronicle,* March 5, 1966.

7. Martin Wyant, "Batavia Goes Out, 93–81, at Aurora East," *Chicago Tribune,* March 12, 1966.

3. From Kitten to Cat

1. This passage is contained in Theodore Roosevelt's "Citizenship in a Republic" speech, delivered on April 23, 1910, in Paris, France. The speech is also known as "The Man in the Arena."

2. John McGill, "Wildcats Overwhelm Georgia 104–73 as Jaracz, Casey Star," *Lexington (Ky.) Herald,* January 16, 1968.

3. Rick Bailey, "McGuire's Words, Antics, Inspire Issel, Wildcats to Mideast Victory," *Lexington (Ky.) Herald-Leader,* March 16, 1968.

4. John McGill, "Buckeyes Stun UK 82–81 for Mideast Title," *Lexington (Ky.) Herald,* March 17, 1968.

5. "Kareem Abdul-Jabbar Details Passing on 1968 Olympics in New Book," NBC Sports, May 22, 2017, https://www.nbcsports.com/olympics/news/kareem-abdul-jabbar-olympics-boycott (accessed December 20, 2024).

4. First Steps Toward Forever

1. Philippians 4:4–5, New International Version.

2. John McGill, "Wisconsin Halts Kentucky Rally, Triumphs 69–65," *Lexington (Ky.) Leader,* January 1, 1969.

3. John McGill, "Marquette Sends UK Stumbling Out of NCAA," *Lexington (Ky.) Herald,* March 14, 1969.

4. "Group Purchases Control of Boone Fried Chicken," *Lexington (Ky.) Herald-Leader,* July 30, 1969.

5. "SEC Seeks Injunction in Boone Chicken Suit," *Lexington (Ky.) Herald-Leader,* July 10, 1970.

6. John McGill, "Issel Drills in 53 Points as Wildcats Roar 120–85," *Lexington (Ky.) Herald,* February 8, 1970.

7. John McGill, "Dolphins Tip Foul-Plagued Kentucky 106–100 in NCAA," *Lexington (Ky.) Herald-Leader,* March 15, 1070.

5. Life as a Colonel

1. Gary Schultz, "Stars Outlast Colonels, Grab ABA Title 131–121," *Louisville (Ky.) Courier-Journal,* May 19, 1971.

2. Gary Schultz, "MVP Issel, McDaniels Fuel ABA East Surge," *Louisville (Ky.) Courier-Journal,* January 30, 1972.

3. Merlynn Nielsen, "Fog Furnishes Cosby Jokes," *Deseret News,* February 6, 1973.

4. "Colonels Tip Cougars to Even Series at 3–3," *Louisville (Ky.) Courier-Journal,* April 22, 1973.

5. Jim Terhune, "Bye Bye Cougars, Hello Pacers," *Louisville (Ky.) Courier Journal,* April 25, 1973.

6. Keith F. Overpeck, "McGinnis Cuffs Colonels as Pacers Take Title," *Louisville (Ky.) Courier-Journal,* May 13, 1973.

6. Finally, a Championship

1. Matt Frassica, "Remembering the '74 Tornado," *Louisville (Ky.) Courier-Journal,* April 2, 2014.

2. Dave Kindred, "Colonels Take ABA Championship with 110–105 Win over Pacers," *Louisville (Ky.) Courier-Journal,* May 23, 1975.

3. Keith F. Overpeck, "At Last, Colonels the Kings!" *Louisville (Ky.) Courier-Journal,* May 23, 1975.

4. Knowles Adkisson, "Silna Settles Longtime NBA Dispute for $500M," *Malibu Times,* April 16, 2014, https://web.archive.org/web/20171219221043/http://www.malibutimes.com/news/article_7a49933a-c573-11e3-95ee-001a4bcf887a.html (accessed May 16, 2025).

5. Jeannine Mancini, "Two Regular Brothers Netted $800 Million from the NBA in History's 'Greatest Sports Deal,'" *Yahoo! Finance,* November 14, 2023, https://finance.yahoo.com/news/two-regular-brothers-netted-800-174101166.html (accessed May 16, 2025).

7. My Journey in the Mile High City

1. "Looking Back at an Unforgettable Holiday—Denver's Christmas Eve Blizzard of 1982," https://www.thorntonweather.com/blog/thornton-weather/looking-back-at-an-unforgettable-holiday-denvers-christmas-eve-blizzard-of-1982/ (accessed April 22, 2025).

2. "Robert Travaglini, Inducted 2000," Colorado Sports Hall of Fame, https://www.coloradosports.org/hall-of-fame/athletes/2000-inductees/robert-travaglini/ (accessed February 24, 2025).

3. Mike Lopresti, "40 Years After First Bird vs. Magic Showdown, 1979 Indiana State Team Celebrates Iconic NCAA Tournament Run," NCAA, January 20, 2019, https://www.ncaa.com/news/basketball-men/article/2019-01-20/40-years-after-first-bird-vs-magic-showdown-1979-indiana-state (accessed May 20, 2025).

4. Sam McManis, "The Last Shootout for Dan Issel," *Los Angeles Times,* May 19, 1985.

9. From Court to Clipboard

1. Phil Taylor, "Its All Up for Grabs: The Inexperienced and Unheralded Nuggets Snuffed the Mighty Sonics and Helped Turn the NBA Playoffs into a Free-for-All," *Sports Illustrated,* May 16, 1994.

2. "Sturm Gets Avs and Nuggets," July 27, 1999, CBS News, https://www.cbsnews.com/news/sturm-gets-avs-and-nuggets/ (accessed March 22, 2025).

3. "Wal-Mart Heir Kroenke Reaches Agreement," Monday, April 24, 2000, ESPN News, https://www.espn.com/gen/news/2000/0424/499222.html (accessed March 22, 2025).

10. Lost Joy

1. John Mossman, "Nuggets Suspend Issel," *Fort Collins Coloradoan,* December 13, 2001.

2. "Issel Accepts Buyout, Resigns from Nuggets," ESPN, https://www.espn.com/nba/news/2001/1222/1300423.html (accessed March 28, 2025).

3. 1 Timothy 6:10, New International Version.

4. Luke 14:11, New International Version.

Epilogue

1. "ABA All-Time Team," Basketball Reference, https://www.basketball-reference.com/awards/aba_all_time_team.html?sr&utm_source=direct&utm_medium=Share&utm_campaign=ShareTool#stats (accessed July 3, 2025).

About the Authors

Dan Issel, known as one of the most durable and dedicated players in basketball history, played in over twelve hundred professional games and missed only twenty-four throughout his entire career. Nicknamed "The Horse," Issel was the embodiment of consistency and toughness, building his legacy on a no-nonsense, blue-collar work ethic. His offensive game was forceful and dependable, featuring strong post moves and a reliable fifteen-foot jumper.

At the University of Kentucky, under the legendary coach Adolph Rupp, Issel set twenty-three school records, including marks for most career points and rebounds. He led the Wildcats to three Southeastern Conference titles and, during his senior season, averaged 33.9 points per game. He elevated that average to 36 points in the postseason, powering Kentucky to the Elite Eight.

Issel went on to a fifteen-year professional career in the ABA and NBA with the Kentucky Colonels and the Denver Nuggets. Upon retiring, he was the Nuggets' all-time leading rebounder and a central figure in the team's history. Issel later returned to the franchise in leadership roles, serving two stints as head coach and also working as general manager. In 1993, he was inducted into the Naismith Memorial Basketball Hall of Fame.

Issel and his wife, Cheri, have two children and five grandchildren. They live in Highlands Ranch, Colorado.

When he's not writing about health and medicine by day or attending concerts by musicians who inspire him, award-winning journalist Doug

Brunk follows the Kentucky Wildcats men's basketball program—a passion he developed during his childhood in Wilmore, Kentucky.

His work has been syndicated by the *Los Angeles Times*, and he is the author of *Wildcat Memories: Inside Stories from Kentucky Basketball Greats*, *Forty Minutes to Glory: Inside the Kentucky Wildcats' 1978 Championship Season*, and coauthor with Jack Givens of *They Call Me Goose: My Life in Kentucky Basketball and Beyond*.

He holds journalism degrees from Point Loma Nazarene University and the S. I. Newhouse School of Public Communications at Syracuse University and lives in San Diego with his wife and their rescue terrier mix.